Camilla

An Intimate Portrait

REBECCA TYRREL

 SHORT BOOKS

This edition first published in 2004 by
Short Books
15 Highbury Terrace
London N5 1UP

10 9 8 7 6 5 4 3 2 1

PICTURE CREDITS
Jacket: Don Features
Mono Plates: Topham Pictures Point, Don Features, Rex Features,
Hulton Getty, Corbis (Matthew Polak, Tim Graham)
Joan Wakeham, Camera Press, PA (Barry Batchelor, Stefan Rousseau,
Sean Dempsey, John Stillwell, Matthew Fearn, Melville)
Every effort has been made to trace copyright holders
and we apologize in advance for any unintentional
omission. We would be pleased to insert the appropriate
acknowledgement in any subsequent edition.

A CIP catalogue record for this book
is available from the British Library.

ISBN 1-904095-53-4

Printed by Bookmarque Ltd, Croydon, Surrey

For Kate

Chapter One

O ne hot summer evening in 1991 an ordinary
44-year-old Englishwoman plumped some
cushions for a 42-year-old man who had broken
his arm playing polo. The break had been a bad
one and, immediately after the accident, after he
had been rushed in great pain to hospital, the bone
had been reset in the wrong position. Now, a few
weeks and two more agonising trips to hospital
later, the man was still in pain and he was fed up.
He wasn't a good patient; he was used to getting
his own way. He was hot and bothered. There was
only one person he could tolerate having near him
when he was feeling like this and that was the
woman who was leaning across him now, reaching
for the cushions behind him in order to plump
them and make him more comfortable. It was such

a kindly, motherly, even wifely gesture. Nobody else did things like this for him.

The cushion-plumper wasn't his mother or his wife, though, and when, just as she was kissing him on the top of his head, his real wife did suddenly appear in the doorway, off the plumper scurried – disappeared through a French window, into her car and off down the drive, back to her own house.

It wasn't the first time the wife had found the other woman there. It was no big deal that she had this time. The marriage was over. But the wife was still angry and she was the confrontational sort, so her rival didn't stick around to witness the row that always followed.

Everybody heard about these goings on. This cushion-plumping incident was just one of the many, many little and not so little moments that everyone in the world would get to hear of when the wife told her story to a journalist one year later. It was the story of how she, Lady Diana Spencer, had married the Prince of Wales but he had never properly loved her. Instead he loved another woman – Camilla Parker Bowles – married with two children, with a shared interest in horses and the countryside, and who lived just down the road from the Prince and Princess's country house, near enough to pop along at a moment's notice for some motherly/wifely cushion-plumping.

It was such a small, insignificant gesture, to plump his cushions, and yet it was read about as far as five and half thousand miles away – in the *San Francisco Chronicle*, for example. The American press, knowing the Brits' 'Carry On' approach to sex, speculated as to whether cushion-plumping might or might not be a euphemism for something rude. And while this was quite funny and risqué, the truth was that even at this relatively early stage in the unravelling of the Prince of Wales's gruesome mismatch of a marriage to Lady Diana Spencer, readers in San Francisco would have had some inkling as to what Mrs Parker Bowles had been doing. It would have been absolutely in character for her to be plumping cushions, if not entirely proper given that those cushions were not officially hers to plump. They are not officially hers to plump even now, thirteen years later, but they might be one day, and that is why this ordinary woman is really quite extraordinary after all.

People who know Camilla say they think of her as someone they are drawn to – a nice-natured, charismatic, uncomplicated, robust, outgoing girl (Note: those who inhabit Camilla's world have a habit of referring to women as 'girls' regardless of whether they are above or below 50 years of age.) The novelist Jilly Cooper, who has been a friend of Camilla's for many years, says, 'I adore her and she is a terrific laugh and I don't know anybody who cheers one up more than she does.'

It is pretty much what they all say about her. Someone else, who doesn't see a great deal of her these days but who used to have her to stay at her house in the country, says, in a raspy, cigarettey voice rather similar to Camilla's own, 'She is a frightfully nice person. She had frightfully nice parents. She is a very jolly girl. She is simply someone about whom there is nothing bad to say.'

Of course, people do say bad things about her. In January 1997, during a Carlton Television monarchy debate, a British studio audience booed and hissed like a football crowd at the very mention of Camilla's name. There are millions of people – dwindling millions – but nevertheless millions, who still remember how they loved Diana and cherish their memory of her. Some people still post poems and eulogies to her on the railings of Kensington Palace; they think Camilla is an old haddock, a trout; they agree with the newspaper which compared her to a horse after Diana supposedly said her husband's lover had the face of a mare and the rump of a stallion; they asked who you'd rather sleep with, the horse or the princess; they lapped up that embarrassing, loving, intrusive Camillagate tape. Camilla is the wicked witch of the West Country, a marriage-breaker. She smells; her house is unhygienic. (It was supposedly the mischievous Diana – who also called her 'The Rottweiler' – who put this last piece of propaganda about, after a driver who had been into Camilla's kitchen reported back that it didn't smell too good.) The typical cuckolded wife, Diana both wanted and didn't want to know about Camilla, and those who reported back to her would have been kind. They would have given her lovely, satisfying little snippets like 'Camilla smells'.

'Mirror mirror on the wall, who is the most fragrant of them all?' the Princess might have asked in this fairytale gone wrong. 'You are

Princess of the People, Queen of Hearts. But not of *his* heart, not of your Prince's heart. He cannot properly love you, because he loves Camilla, and there just isn't room for you and your young girl's problems.'

And it wasn't just Diana who said bad things about Camilla. Even Mrs Parker Bowles, at her most self-deprecating, has said, upon seeing a photo of herself in the paper, 'Thirteen double chins and me with my head in my handbag.'

The truth, though, lies – as it usually does – somewhere in the middle. Camilla must be a loyal and frightfully nice person, at least to her friends, because no one has gone cantering to the press to say otherwise. But she must also be held at least partially responsible for breaking up that marriage, which may never have been the fairytale we were sold but which was a marriage of a nation's Prince to a childlike bride and should therefore have been sacrosanct, no matter how big a storm was being whipped up by the difficult childlike bride. No matter how hard she was to handle.

So Camilla must be a bit wicked to have taken part in the dashing of all those hopes – in merely being *available* so that Charles didn't have to knuckle down and see it through, and nurture and care for his poor troubled wife.

And because the goddess Diana, who suffered by Camilla's actions, was peachy-skinned and beautiful – a compassionate, radiant, suffering girl – Camilla perforce looks dowdy in comparison, possibly even a bit haddock-like. She has a horsey chin and someone who knows her once said that there have been times when she hasn't washed after hunting, that she was happy to leap, still sweating, off a horse and into an evening dress without having a bath. It was a good friend who said this, incidentally, and he was intending it as a compliment, comparing rough-and-ready, game girl Camilla to pristine, high-maintenance, neurotic Diana. Someone else remarked, while comparing Camilla to the Princess, 'If she has a problem, rather than go and see a therapist, she is a lot more likely to go fox-hunting, come back, put some rum in her tea and have some scrambled egg to eat.'

It is unlikely that she would bother to wash her hands before making that scrambled egg, but what matter? Camilla isn't the type to wash her hands after handling an animal, or even just stroking an animal – or at least she certainly never used to be in the days before she became so fond of frosted highlights and French manicures. People who live like Camilla lived then don't worry about getting dog drool over the steak-and-kidney-pie filling and they have black lines under their fingernails from weeding round the taddle stones in the front of the house or plunging their hands into buckets of steaming bran mash on a winter's morning. People like Camilla come from good, solid four-square homes in the countryside with untidy rows of muddy boots by the back door.

It's a life that sounds so nice and comfortable and easy, one in which the only real worry is how to get the dog hairs off the sofa cushions... So why did she have to go and complicate it? Was she mad? Was she driven by raging, self-promoting ambition, or was she simply in love with Prince Charles? Does she, to this day, honestly, as her friend Patty Palmer-Tomkinson once put it, 'just want to breathe the same air'? Is this the story of a jolly nice, down-to-earth girl who got involved with a jolly confused Prince of Wales?

Chapter Two

Camilla's childhood house was a former recto-ry called The Laines, a fair-sized hotchpotch of a place opposite Plumpton racecourse in East Sussex, with ivy on the garden walls and bees buzzing around the cotoneaster. There was a large, velvety lawn for croquet, a geranium-scented con-servatory and a gravelled sweep in through brick gateposts. This wasn't the first marital home for Camilla's parents, Major Bruce Shand and his wife, the Honourable Rosalind Shand, née Cubitt. They started their marriage in a rental, the Old Manor, another version of The Laines just a few miles down the road in Westdean. They also had a house in London, in South Kensington.

They were married in January 1946 and Camilla was born eighteen months later at seven o'clock in the morning on 17th July 1947 at King's College Hospital in London. She is sixteen months older than her prince, whose own birth on 14th November 1948 was posted on the railings outside Buckingham Palace just before midnight. His arrival was heralded by a royal birthday salute from the warships of His Majesty's naval fleet around the world and the fountains in Trafalgar Square ran blue for a boy.

There is an irresistible historical symmetry that lies at the heart of the saga of Camilla and Charles – Alice Keppel, Camilla's maternal great-grand-mother was the official mistress of Edward VII in the days when princes and kings had official mis-tresses or *maîtresses en titre*, as the tabloids have taken to referring to Mrs Parker Bowles when they are not calling her a paramour. This Keppel coin-cidence is so irresistible that Camilla, as the famous early part of her love story goes, exploited it suggestively with a nudge and a wink and a wry, seductive smile during an early encounter with Prince Charles. 'My great-grandmother and your great-great-grandfather were lovers. So how about it?' she proposed.

She might also have mentioned to the Prince that her paternal grandfather was a respected authority on architecture, and that in some of the articles and books he had published there was a lovely, irresistible, monstrous carbuncle link. But probably not, because this coincidence would have hinted at a rather more dusty, bookish relationship than she apparently had in mind. As it was, the Sainsbury wing of the National Gallery had yet to be built and in those early days of Charles and Camilla, the playboy prince was more interested in pretty girls at polo matches than preservation and Poundbury.

Camilla's architecture-loving grandfather knew a great deal not just about buildings but also wine, food and, it must be imagined, wives because he was married four times. 'We had a strange relationship,' said Camilla's father, Bruce Shand, 'I never saw him until I was 38 – apart from at my grandfather's funeral when I was eighteen.'

His name was Phillip Morton Shand. He was always known as P. Morton Shand and the story of his life is a Wodehousian gem, which, oddly but happily for researchers into Camilla's forebears, was written up in 1995 by William Whittam. Whittam had to work hard for his book (which was never published), for his subject left very little biographical detail behind him.

He did, however, leave some of his works – *The Book of Food*, *A Book of French Wine* and *A Book of Wine*. He left his translations of books by Walter Gropius – German into English – and another translation of a play by Arthur Schnitzler. He also left three children by three of his four wives, although the one who knew her father best, the third child, Elspeth (now Lady Howe, wife of the former Chancellor of the Exchequer, Lord Howe of Aberavon), decided not to speak to Whittam. Bruce Shand, on the other hand, the only son of P. Morton Shand, was helpful, imparting what information and insight he could. His other half-sister Sylvia also gave her side of the story.

Born in Kensington in 1888, P. Morton Shand was the only child of Augusta and Alexander Shand. Alexander was a writer, author of a book on psychology called *The Foundations of Character*. He was also a barrister who rarely practised any law because he was wealthy enough not to have to work. His merchant family had made a fortune in the Glasgow calico trade.

Phillip was sent to Eton, won prizes for German and Divinity and then went up to King's College, Cambridge, where he listened to

Strindberg and wore 'daring neckties'. 'Shand was a man of mercurial temperament,' King's journal noted following his death. 'He had strong likes and dislikes. His detestation of port was well known; whisky he considered a poison fit only for persons of depraved tastes; and he was really offended by the more vulgar forms of ugliness.'

After Cambridge, Shand studied at the Sorbonne. He is described as 'an insatiable Lothario', and 'a dilettante', 'a linguist and a dazzling conversationalist'. For a while it was thought that he might enter the consular service and although his war records have disappeared, he did at some stage serve in the Royal Artillery. But by the time of his first marriage in 1916, to Edith Marguerite Harrington, he was working, rather uninspiringly for such an apparently rip-roaring sort of man, as a clerk in the War Office.

Edith was an accountant's daughter from Hammersmith and Bruce, the son she had with P. Morton Shand, was born exactly nine months after the wedding. No sooner had the war ended, though, than P. Morton Shand bolted off without his wife or child to travel around Europe and there womanise, spend his considerable allowance and continue being the erudite and dazzling conversationalist. The neglected Edith petitioned for divorce on the grounds of adultery. A year later she married an army officer called Herbert Tippet, whom Camilla's father referred to in a book he published in 1990 called *Previous Engagements*, an account of his own military career.

In it he describes his childhood as being 'rather *mouvementé*', and Tippet is mentioned briefly as someone who 'although not a regular soldier, had fought with gallantry in the 1914 war and had retained a taste for the army, with considerable knowledge of its uniforms, history and traditions. Perhaps some of this rubbed off on me.'

Meanwhile, back in 1920, within weeks of his divorce, P. Morton Shand had married again. This time it was to, Alys Fabre-Tonerre, the daughter of a Frenchman who was a police superintendent in India. Fifteen days later, their daughter, Sylvia, was born.

Three years later, Shand was off again, this time alighting upon the daughter of a notary from Lyon called Georgette Avril. Alys duly petitioned for divorce, Shand married Georgette, his third wife, and appeared to settle down for a while. He wrote profusely about wine, food and architecture, making the kind of pronouncements which proved that he could not be said to be in the vanguard of the feminist movement. His most famous and impractical was: 'A woman who cannot make soup should not be allowed to marry.'

Soon, however, he became so engrossed in his work that whether his wife could make soup or not didn't matter – he thoroughly neglected her. He was divorced for the third time in 1931 and the petition was heard in the high court where the presiding judge, a Lord Merivale, described Shand as 'a peculiarly shameless litigant'. During the summing up he mulled, 'There is, of course, no statutory means of preventing a man like the respondent from playing the havoc apparently he is capable of playing.' Merivale then went on to remark that 'a little wholesome publicity' might limit Shand's activities, 'at least in this country'. The *Daily Mail* duly obliged but this didn't stop Shand from remarrying just eight days later. To be fair, he did manage to stick with Sybil Slee, an accountant's daughter from Croydon, the former wife of a commander in the Royal Navy. The soup was obviously drinkable and the marriage was longlasting if not exactly blissful. Elspeth, now Lady Howe, was their only child.

Shand's success with women is put down to his

brilliant conversation. 'He never stopped talking,' Bruce Shand told Whittam, 'he was a very good raconteur.' One of his greatest friends was John Betjeman. And Betjeman's daughter, Candida Lycett Green – who is very close to Camilla Parker Bowles – described P. Morton Shand as kind and perceptive. So not the complete libertine he might seem. Or perhaps the Shands have the knack of making friends with people who close ranks and can only do compliments. It was in a letter Shand wrote to Betjeman that the carbuncular link with Prince Charles was revealed. As Camilla's father explained, 'By preaching the very avant-garde form of architecture, [in the 1920s], he had rather sown the dragon's teeth.'

'London is now a nightmare of hideous and shoddy Americanised buildings [wrote P. Morton Shand to Betjeman] …that it has reduced me to a state of mental debility in which I can scarcely credit what my eyes confront …I have frightful nightmares, and no wonder, for I am haunted by a gnawing sense of guilt in having, in however minor and obscure a degree, helped to bring about, any-how encourage and praise, the embryo searchings that have now materialised into a monster neither of us could have foreseen; contemporary architecture (the piling up of gigantic children's toy bricks in utterly dehumanised and meaningless forms), art and all that, it is no longer funny, it is frightening.'

Some of Prince Charles's hand-wringing and whingeing about architecture must surely have been inspired by this letter. Perhaps he has read it. It seems hard, in fact, to believe from the familiar prose style that he has not.

By 1937 P. Morton Shand's wife was also writing to her husband's friend John Betjeman. She was begging him to find her husband a full-time job away from the house, a plea which suggests that he was not at all easy to live with. But Shand stayed at home and wrote for a variety of publications: *the Listener*, *the Architectural Review* and a magazine called *Concrete Way*, the official journal for the Federation of Concrete Manufacturers.

Major Shand has said that he feels his father's greatest achievement was his wine writing, but perhaps this is simply the subject the son has a greater affinity with. In the early 1950s, the Major and a friend took over a wine merchant's business in South Audley Street called Block, Grey & Block on the site of what is now Harry's Bar, a modern-day haunt of Charles and Camilla and their friends.) 'In those days,' said Major Shand, 'nobody had written about wine. Now we get five books published about it every day, don't we? But then he was rather a voice crying in the wilderness.'

He must be less proud however, if not exactly ashamed, of his father's other legacy – the fractured family, disparate web of half-sisters and step-parents. He told William Whittam, 'I don't think I'd ever have seen him had my wife not said that the children (Camilla, Annabel and Mark) should meet their grandfather.' P. Morton Shand died aged 72 in 1960 and towards the end of his father's life Bruce saw him from time to time. He said they got on 'not too badly'.

***

Like his father, Major Shand, although by all accounts a much kinder and less flighty man, has an air of Wodehousian Woosterishness about him. His grandson, Ben Elliot, Camilla's nephew, says, 'Major Bruce Shand is a magnificent, graceful, elegant man.' He must be one of the few people left on this earth who really does say 'What?' at the end of all his sentences; he is also the sort of fellow who refers to young women as 'fillies'.

He has favourite anecdotes, which he tells and retells, like the one about the royal standard and the French lady's handbag. Bruce Shand served for sixteen years in the Queen's Household, as clerk of the Cheque and adjutant of the Yeoman of the Guard. 'We were always dressed for the Battle of Waterloo,' he once said. And one of his tasks while thus dressed was to carry the standard on State occasions and lower it when the Queen passed through the Royal Gallery. One day when he was doing this he accidentally hooked the handbag of a French visitor on the end of the flagstaff. When Major Shand tells the story, he finishes off with 'That was dramatic, what? The Queen was very amused by the whole thing.'

At the time of Camilla's birth he had been recently demobilised. In 1937 he had joined the 12th Royal Lancers, a cavalry regiment, from Sandhurst and 53 years later he published his book. It is a bracing, rousing, touching but at the same time no-nonsense account of his military career and on the flyleaf it says that Major Shand chose the 12th Royal Lancers 'as much because he liked hunting and riding as for any more martial inclination'. *Previous Engagements* is a collection of 'young man's narratives, in the mood of class and period'. It tells how, by the time Major Shand was wounded and captured in North Africa in 1942, he had won the MC twice.

The flyleaf observes that his sort of apparently *laissez-faire* attitude in the British Army before the Second World War might have been expected to improve Hitler's chances, but in the event the Germans found that the likes of the author and his friends had a perplexing 'knack of rising to the occasion'. This is the tone in which the book is written – self-deprecating and not taking one's silly old self too terribly seriously even in the worst possible of times.

Major Shand is bluff and honest and his ex-army friends have names like 'Stinker' Dowell, 'Dozy' Willis, 'Dusty' Smith, 'Shaggy' Ransome and 'Bloody' Mike Blakiston-Houston who was particularly known for his language, which was said to rival that of the Duke of Cambridge.

It is telling that up to this point in *Previous Engagements* there is no reference to the Duke of Cambridge or his language and it backs up something else the flyleaf says, that the memoir was written primarily to evoke vivid memories amongst the Major's friends and contemporaries who would all, doubtless, have known exactly how much the Duke swore. They would have laughed gales about it and slapped each other's backs all over town while drinking at Boodle's club in St James's where the Major and many of his friends and army contemporaries were members. Here, and in restaurants and bars and at the Four Hundred club, the young Bruce Shand ran up bills he couldn't pay which were settled later by a committee of friends – not an unusual thing in these sorts of circles where you looked after your own, much as you do when you are under the cosh and fighting together for your country. Friends of Bruce's father, P. Morton Shand, had done the same.

Camilla's father's book gives insight into the kind of person he was and, by all accounts still is, and because father and daughter are so close and fond of each other we therefore learn something about Camilla, too.

In an interview he gave to a newspaper in 1993 in the wake of the Camillagate furore, Major Shand refused to comment on his daughter's relationship with the Prince of Wales but was quoted on the equally important subject of hunting and how badly turned out some of those who hunt seem to be these days.

'We can't have people turning up as if they've been wearing the same pyjamas for a month,' he said. On the subject of hunt saboteurs he argued with a spectacular but impressive lack of logic, 'Overpopulation is the problem. Everybody getting on top of everybody else's toes. Not enough room to mind your own business. And that doesn't just apply to hunting.'

Point taken. Except that who the Prince of Wales might or might not marry is, like it or not, everybody's business. It should also be noted that, while Camilla has in the past looked as if she has just spent the night in one of her dog's baskets, she always looks very well laundered when out hunting. Like most caricature bluff majors, though, Bruce Shand seems to be happiest when talking about his military career. He described the moment when he was wounded and taken prisoner as 'Rather a dreary performance. I ran into a group of German vehicles. The only distinction was that it was said to be Rommel's HQ.'

He punctuated his story with some wheezy gentleman's club laughter. 'I got hit in the face [he has the scar beneath his eye] and the leg. The agony came later.' Is he brave? 'Don't think so.

There's no point getting in a flap on these occasions. What?'

So, like father, like daughter. Not long ago, laid-back, easy-going Camilla told a friend that she never misses a night's sleep. This is an extraordinary admission for someone whose minutest actions create a butterfly effect and end up being analysed in a newspaper in San Francisco, and whose not-so-minute actions reverberate and reverberate until a future king's marriage is broken, the people's princess is dead and a nation is left wondering who their next sovereign will be and who will be his queen. But then they are made of stern stuff these Shands. They are not at all 'invertebrates', as the Major once described himself.

Chapter Three

In 2002 a short newspaper item revealed that an American genealogist, William Addams Reitwiesner, had found that Camilla Parker Bowles's great-grandparents from nine generations ago were ancestors not just of Madonna but also of Céline Dion. Camilla and Madonna have a Monsieur Zacharie Cloutier (1617-1708) in common with each other, while Camilla and Céline Dion descend from Monsieur Jean Guyon (1619-1694).

This is the kind of pleasingly meaningless but gripping stuff that will be dredged up and published about you if you do something as high-profile as having an extra-marital affair with the heir to the throne. So imagine what happens if you have an ancestor who also had an extra-marital affair with an heir to the throne who then became a king. Camilla Parker Bowles is already gripping enough for her own love life but she is made even more fascinating because of that of her great-grandmother, Alice Keppel – wife of George Keppel, official mistress of King Edward VII.

One early boyfriend of Camilla's, Kevin Burke, says the Keppel link played a major part in the early days; that when Charles and Camilla first met, or at least when she propositioned him with the very fact of it, the royal adultery issue was 'talismanic'. She was always mentioning it.

Had the young Camilla spent a childhood on her mother's knee, begging to be told over and over again the story of her great-grandmother who was a very special friend of a king? Perhaps she had. It is not entirely impossible, given that a favourite family anecdote – the faintly rude one that made the children snigger and snort – was the one where Mrs Keppel would say, 'My job is to curtsy first and then jump into bed.' It doesn't look as if this juiciest of all pieces of family gossip imaginable (although Camilla's scandal has in the event been so much juicier) was exactly hidden, but neither does it seem to have been treated with any particular awe or respect. Indeed school-friends have said that Camilla bragged about being related to Alice Keppel. She particularly talked about the holidays the King and Alice would take together each year in Biarritz and the fact that Alice was inner circle enough to be summoned to the King's deathbed – in other words, her great-grandmother was pretty much as close as you can get to royalty. So there, beat that.

Camilla's parents, particularly Rosalind Shand, cannot have been too fazed, then, when their daughter started bringing her new boyfriend, Charles Windsor, home to Sussex in the early 1970s. They certainly wouldn't have rushed around with the whitewash or starched any napkins in his honour – although they may well have plumped some cushions. And they might have been a bit worried that it would all end in tears, or that the press might find out, because their eldest daughter had been offered and had apparently accepted the role of royal sex-motherer.

This was an unofficial job and the person who took it on was absolutely crucial to the development of the heir to the throne – or so Lord Mountbatten, Prince Charles's surrogate grandfather, believed. The sex-motherer, ideally a nice girl with a good bit of experience in the bedroom department, was to perform a service keeping Charles happy until the one with 'no past', the marriage material, came along. Camilla could never have married Charles herself because, according to Mountbatten's beautifully anachronistic and chauvinistic motto, 'A bedded can't be wedded'. This only applied to girls, however. Boys were supposed to get on with the bedding as soon as their hormones allowed, while the wedding was supposed to follow a few years later if and when they could find a virgin.

What Mountbatten said, or rather wrote, in a letter to his favourite prince was: 'I believe in a case like yours, that a man should sow his wild oats and have as many affairs as he can before settling down. But for a wife he should choose a sweet-charactered girl before she meets anyone else she might fall for.'

Camilla was not the sweet-charactered girl he had in mind – she was the raw material and, at the time she was seeing Prince Charles, she was two-timing him with Andrew Parker Bowles, a dashing lieutenant in the Royal Horse Guards who, in the summer of 1971, was away serving his country in Germany. Camilla's parents would have understood that in her own special way

Camilla was serving her country too.

The Honourable Rosalind doesn't appear to have been a prudish or particularly strict woman. Photographs show her to be a neat sort of person in her pearls and her tidy sweaters and cardigans. She was elegant, certainly, and she seems to have done things properly and grandly, as Camilla's 1965 'coming-out' at Searcy's in Knightsbridge proves. The throwing open of The Laines for Conservative party fund-raising fêtes says a lot too. Rosalind was a busy, country-drawing-room sort of person, a herbaceous-border type who wore brooches and had neat hair like the Queen's.

She was young, just 24, when she married Bruce Shand in 1946 at St Paul's Church in Knightsbridge. Her mother, Sonia, was Alice Keppel's 'other' daughter, the sister we know little about in comparison to Violet (Trefusis) – who, so hopelessly, loved Vita Sackville-West.

You'd think with all these bits of all these ancestors, all mixed up in the genealogical trug basket and scattered through a couple of generations – bits of P. Morton Shand with his quartet of wives; bits of his father, the amateur psychologist and author of The Foundations of Character; bits of Alice; and bits of highly strung, difficult Violet

– that the end result would be something a bit more complicated, a bit more hard to manage, more romantic than good old countrywoman, Victoria sponge and rhododendrons, riding-to-hounds Camilla.

But perhaps the charisma of Alice, the rebellious bohemianism of Violet and the dilettante in P. Morton Shand parade themselves in her after all – in the wry humour and gregariousness that her jolly, loyal friends all commend her so highly for. One can go along with this theory until, of course, you learn that she shares a love of the Goons and practical jokes involving elastic bands bursting out of envelopes in common with her blue-blooded boyfriend.

And it would be a mistake to think that Camilla's interest in watercolours demonstrates any particular artiness or Bohemian oneness with her ancestors, for watercolour painting is a home counties pastime – as home counties as a conservatory extension and a barbecue terrace, as Tory woman as a headscarf. The realistic landscapes they paint and hang in their houses are the naff side of Prince Charles and Camilla, the proof that if they could be reincarnated as plain and un-famous Mr and Mrs Windsor of Chippenham they would spend their retirement afternoons watching *Watercolour Challenge* with Hannah Gordon on BBC1 and *Countdown*.

Camilla's cousin Judith Keppel, the gently eccentric but geekily clever winner of *Who Wants to Be A Millionaire*, is perhaps more the sort of descendant you would have expected from the Keppel line. As it is, Camilla's mother, Rosalind, whose maiden name was Cubitt (the Anglo-Saxon meaning of which is apparently 'elbow'), seems to fit more with her paternal side. Her father, Roland Cubitt, who became Lord Ashcombe around the time of Rosalind's marriage to Bruce in 1946, was descended from two Thomas Cubitts. One was a tenant farmer in Buxton in Norfolk in the 1760s. The other, later one was a carpenter with ambition. He fathered twelve children and built up his business until, demonstrating quite remarkable entrepreneurial skill for a 'penniless son of a Coltishall farmer', he found himself building much of Belgravia. He became an advisor to Prince Albert and was recommended for a peerage but died before his big day at the palace. The title was conferred instead upon his son George and it was George's grandson Roland who married Sonia Keppel, Alice's daughter.

There are people – biographers, historians – who enjoy the symmetry of the royal adultery across the generations so much that they like to believe that Sonia was the daughter of King Edward VII. The timing was right; she was conceived and born when Alice and 'Kingy', as Sonia and Violet knew him, were very close and spending a lot of time promenading in Biarritz together. If Sonia was Kingy's offspring, then that would make Camilla and Charles second cousins once removed.

However, Diana Souhami, a reliable source, author of the minutely researched *Alice and her Daughter* – a biography of Alice and Violet – prefers to believe that Sonia was the legitimate daughter of George Keppel, whose marriage, despite there being three in it, didn't suffer from any overcrowding and was solid and enduring and still spawned offspring. Sonia, writes Souhami, had the Keppel nose and temperament.

Sonia divorced her Cubitt husband in 1947, which was a quite momentous year for the Cubitt/Keppel families because shortly afterwards Alice and George Keppel died – just missing the birth of their new great-granddaughter, Camilla Shand.

If Alice Keppel had lived, what would she have made of her great-granddaughter? She would have been proud of Camilla, surprised at the coincidence, and she would have felt sorry for her that the press these days are so intrusive. If she had simply survived long enough to know Camilla as a child, however, she would have had no surprises at all. Rosalind and Bruce, Camilla's parents, were good solid, family-oriented, charming, likeable, uncomplicated people who gave their children an Enid Blyton, Pony Club, *Mallory Towers* upbringing. Major Shand once said, 'Because of my disruptive childhood, I was very keen to see that my own children had an even run. They all had an agreeable time. I'm proud of them all.'

Rosalind Shand, when once asked about her daughter's relationship with Prince Charles, refused to comment, saying only, 'None of us has ever broken ranks.' And it is that 'no rank breaking' rule, a rule still enforced among friends and family, which is, it would seem, Camilla's strongest card. She has vowed to go to her grave without giving an interview. There are people who are close to her, however, who are given permission to speak of her vaguely and kindly and those – friends of both Camilla and Charles – who will give quotes about how all the Prince and his girl-friend want is to be left alone to be with each other. And there are others, too – aides and spinners – and what they know and say to journalists and biographers tells us a lot about how far Camilla has strayed from the life her parents meant for her when they gave her that 'even run'.

Chapter Four

The Shands had three children, Camilla, Annabel and Mark, enough to fill a house like The Laines with noise, the 'Gawlly gawsh, how *rarelair larvely* Mummy', kind of noise you would imagine post-war children with plums in their mouths making in the summer holidays.

At the time Camilla was born, Major Shand had taken a job as an educational films representative. Like many of their type, members of the squirearchy, both he and the Honourable Mrs Shand had private incomes – the Cubitts were very rich after all that building in the swankier parts of London and Bruce benefited from his calico merchant's ancestors – so there was no immediate need for him to find a job. But he felt he had to.

He was typical of someone just out of the

army, the energetic young major who suddenly finds himself travelling in floor-cleaning products, or as the old joke goes, in ladies' underwear. As one former soldier explains, 'Just out of the army you have no vocational training per se. You might be jolly good at going bravely over the top but you know nothing about Civvy Street. In the outside world people don't instinctively obey orders, there isn't a hierarchy of rank. You are desperate because you hate having nothing to do after being so busy, so you take the first job that comes along.'

Thirty years later, Camilla's ex-husband, Brigadier Andrew Parker Bowles, was reported to have done much the same sort of thing on retiring from the Royal Veterinary Corps. He was said, and it turned out to be untrue but it needn't have been, to have taken a job as a debt collector. If it had been true it would have been a job that Parker Bowles would have acquired through friends. Ex-army people stare blankly like rabbits into the headlights and then they pick up the phone and ask for help. When their friends fail them they go to job agencies. They hate having no support structure.

But Major Shand wasn't an educational films representative for very long. It was in the early

1950s that he and a friend joined Block, Grey & Block, the wine merchant's in South Audley Street. He lived between Sussex and a house in South Kensington, was appointed joint MFH of the Southdown Hunt in 1956 and became so embedded and involved that he was appointed Deputy Lord Lieutenant of East Sussex, the Queen's official representative in the county. The Shands, in other words, were the right sort of people to know. When the man mowing the village green saw the Major on his horse, he'd say, 'Good morning, Squire.'

So Camilla was secure in that rosy-cheeked, tree-climbing, skinny-dipping sort of life and she was certainly grounded enough as a small child to survive her first school. Dumbrells was, by all accounts – mostly tabloid ones which described Camilla as having a 'mop of curls' – an establishment that made Dotheboys Hall look like the Connaught. It was only three miles from The Laines, in a place called Ditchling, but still Camilla boarded. At Dumbrells, which is often described as uncarpeted – as if an uncarpeted school was a dreadful abberation, as if all the other schools in the country at the time were run through with prime, tufted Wilton – the girls, even the infants, were expected to break the proverbial ice on their water bowls. At 6.30 each morning the children, most of them probably missing their mummies, were woken and at 7.30 a bell would ring for some 'violent exercises'. This allegedly continued for a barely believable 29 minutes – the poor little mites.

Dumbrells was founded somewhere between 1880 and 1885 by the three Dumbrell sisters, who, we must assume, dressed in black and looked like Elvira Gulch. The youngest Miss Dumbrell (sounds similar to the nonagenarian Young Mr Grace in *Are You Being Served*?) apparently spoke like a Victorian sampler.

In Camilla's day, though, an ex-pupil called Miss Helen Knowles ran the school. She joined in 1912 and left in 1982 after a remarkable 60-year stint. And when she did leave it was because the school was shut down, possibly a victim of 'Thatcher, Thatcher Milk Snatcher's' education policies. One Old Dumbrellian confirmed to Christopher Wilson, a biographer of Camilla, that discipline was extraordinarily harsh.

'It was decreed that any possession found lying about must then be worn by the culprit for a whole day, including mealtimes. One older girl came to lunch wearing three hats; a younger one was sadly hampered by a large sewing basket tied to her waist.' Small children who misbehaved had to sit under the headmistress's revolving, squeaking chair for an hour. One child, bless her heart, was told to eat a greenfly she had been seen scraping off a lettuce leaf. Other Camilla contemporaries remember the cold, and the fact that there was a large, crucified bat (quite feasibly a Dumbrell ancestor) hanging in the entrance hall of the school.

A teacher from Camilla's time remembers Camilla as 'ever such a pretty girl with blonde hair and perfect manners. She was just ever such a nice, polite little girl. She didn't really stand out in any way from the other children, there was nothing special about her. I would say she was intelligent, hardworking, and had a sweet nature.'

And then there was the school inspector who paid a visit during the time that Camilla was there and was apparently 'dumbstruck' that such an establishment as Dumbrells could exist. 'I used to say that a child who could cope with Dumbrell's could cope with anything,' said someone else who was there at the same time.

These early trials suffered with such vim by the

plucky, mop-haired little Shand girl contrast conveniently for biographers, and dramatically, with Prince Charles's miserable trials by icy washbowl and presumably even more violent exercise at Cheam and later at Gordonstoun. Prince Charles told Jonathan Dimbleby, his authorised biographer, that his school days were like a 'prison sentence... the unhappiest time of my life'. At Cheam he cried himself to sleep and he would 'shudder' with terror throughout the journey there after the holidays. Camilla, by comparison, coped. She was the child who grew into the woman who never misses a night's sleep. Good, solid, grounded Camilla with her advanced cushion-plumping techniques.

***

Meanwhile, at home at The Laines, for Camilla at least, life would have revolved around the Pony Club and the hunt. She owned her own pony by the time she was five and she went to Pony Club camp. A florid-faced man called Broderick Munro Wilson, someone who knew Camilla as a child and who could have been Mastermind champion with his specialist subject 'Camilla – Toddler to

Puberty', has spoken many times about how the Shands, as well as welcoming the local hunt at The Laines for meets would host events known as Duckling Dances. 'The girls would have party dresses with sashes from a place called the White House in Bond Street and the boys would be in dinner jackets,' recalls the invaluable Munro Wilson.

'There would be jelly and ice-cream and lots of organised dancing, all the boys on one side and all the girls on the other. My mother told me to dance with all the girls, not just the pretty ones. I danced with Camilla, although I never went out with her. Sometimes there would be a three-piece band and sometimes the music would come from a wind-up gramophone. There was no snogging in the cupboards. It was all very polite. There is a certain boldness required to riding, hunting and jumping, and that shone through with Camilla.'

Major Shand, six foot three in his moleskin trousers, a tall, imposing, lantern-jawed fellow, 'a classic cavalryman, slim and imperial', reports Munro Wilson, once remarked on the subject of bringing his children up, 'I don't think we had any more problems than anyone else. They've always been quite chatty. There haven't been any inhibitions in their upbringing that I know of.'

One anecdote, told by Camilla's brother Mark Shand when he was attempting to promote a book he had written, proves that things were not always harmonious in the nursery. One night in 1959, aged eight, when he was home for the holidays from Milton Abbey school, Shand determined to murder one of his sisters. Shand has subsequently refused to say whether it was Camilla, then aged twelve, or the ten-year-old Annabel he had it in for. Whoever it was, he says he 'loathed her with an obsessive passion'.

'She was everybody's favourite. She could do no wrong – and, when she did, I was blamed... At midnight I wobbled naked along the moonlit passage to my sister's room and slowly pushed open the door. She was lying in her bed like a giant blancmange, mouth wide open.'

Was it Camilla sleeping so soundly – she who never misses a night's sleep even with a murderous brother lurking in the shadows?

'Camilla was very easy-going,' (Munro Wilson again). 'She was into boys much quicker than other girls of her age. There was this daredevil element in her. She would make the running. She is a girl who has probably always known what she wanted and gone for it.' Someone else, not Munro Wilson this time, once noted rather bizarrely that Annabel was 'not the sort to throw her knickers on the table'. The implication seems clear. Camilla was very much the sort who did.

By the time the Shand children were teenagers they seem to have evolved from Enid Blyton-type children into an Hons and Rebels-ish clan with its in-jokes and secret places. If Camilla did throw her knickers on the table – and it could be that this was just a figure of speech – but, say she did, she would have run the risk that her underwear might have got mixed up with the napery, been mistaken for a napkin perhaps. And it had to be a 'napkin' – never a 'serviette'. Anyone saying 'serviette' or 'toilet' or 'couch' or 'lounge', anyone holding their knife like a pen or saying 'pardon' instead of 'what' would provoke extreme hilarity in the Shand household. Presumably the cleaner or the gardener or the local shopkeeper or the man who mowed the village green or anyone who would have called the Major 'Squire' would have escaped the shaming, but any child or awkward adolescent coming to tea and committing such a social not-nicety would be laughed at after they had left.

A female friend of the family said, 'They [the Shand children] always had an enormous amount of confidence and they had their parents to thank for that. They were loved to death, which was most unusual in their class in those days. The Shands always encouraged them to be themselves... they were raised by praise and it showed. They always seemed much more sophisticated, more at ease with themselves. While we were still dressed like little children, Camilla and Annabel were wearing smart little black sleeveless dresses. They were also very unselfconscious about their bodies. Whereas we spent all our time covering ourselves up and pulling our pullovers down, because we'd had it drummed into us that either we were ugly or that it was vulgar to do otherwise, they wore bikinis. It is not that they had particularly good figures, it was just that they weren't ashamed of being women.'

People say this sort of thing a lot about Camilla – that she is no great shakes to look at but that there is something about her. They said this about Alice Keppel, too. Rebecca West wrote that her 'charm was not in her looks...' She went on to note that Alice possessed a 'noting concerned quality, as if she were a theatre sister in a well-run hospital'. So, Camilla was born of good cushion-plumping stock.

Camilla's peers at Queen's Gate school in South Kensington, where she arrived at the age of ten and where she is remembered for wearing the same hair-style she wears today and for climbing out onto the roof for cigarettes while someone in her thrall kept watch, say that she wasn't particularly pretty or fashionable but that she was popular and managed to get herself noticed. 'Camilla has done an awful lot for plain women,' wrote a female newspaper columnist a few years back and this seems to be confirmed by the recollections of her school peers.

Penelope Fitzgerald, the Booker Prize-winning author, was a teacher at Queen's Gate at the time Camilla was there and although she never actually taught 'Milla', as she was briefly known, because Milla didn't stay on for A levels, Fitzgerald does remember her for her pretty hair and the fact that she excelled at fencing – something that must have made the Major really proud, especially when weighed against her one O level.

Lynn Ripley, an excellent advertisement for the school in that she went on to become the pop singer known as Twinkle – apparently having written her hit single 'Terry' about a young man who died in a motor-bike accident during a French lesson – has many recollections of Milla.

'I always thought she was the coolest girl in school,' she recalls, rather quaintly reverting to the vernacular of the early 1960s. 'I started to wear way-out clothes, but Milla never got out of her twin sets and tweed skirts.' Twinkle maintains that Camilla was a Sloane Ranger before Sloane Rangers were invented which is one in the eye for Lady Di whose early but dubious achievement was to be dubbed the 'Sloane Rangers' Sloane Ranger' in the late 1970s and early 1980s.

Twinkle reached number four in the charts and married the man in the black polo-neck from the Milk Tray advert. They settled down in Cobham, Surrey, had two children and as many coffee creams as they could eat. A very different path from Camilla, then, who headed much further into the home counties – Wiltshire then Gloucestershire – and had an affair with the young man in the kilt from that Royal Family documentary, and while she may never have written a chart hit, she did inspire the former Beatle, Sir Paul McCartney, to come up with the un-funny nickname for her of 'Camilla Park Yer Bowels'.

Twinkle described Camilla as 'Oddly conventional. She didn't seem to mind being different from the others. It was odd in a way, because girls can be cruel, but there was an inner something in Milla that others recognised as stronger.'

The actress Lynn Redgrave was a senior girl when Camilla arrived at Queen's Gate. She said, rather sneerily, 'I think I was the only girl who had a working mother.' She was probably right, though, and she and Twinkle were probably among the very few who went on to have jobs themselves – although Camilla did work briefly for Colefax & Fowler as a secretary/receptionist and her sister Annabel did co-found an interior design business in Dorset. But Camilla's heart wasn't set on a career. Her heart was set upon exactly what it was meant to be set upon – a good marriage, some children, some horses, some dogs, some staff and a kitchen with an Aga in a county ending with the syllable 'shire'.

Annabel was the arty one, the one with the more enquiring mind, who worked hard at school, the one who, on leaving Queen's Gate, went to Florence where both Alice Keppel and her daughter Violet Trefusis had retreated after their newsworthy love affairs. Camilla went abroad, too, briefly, to Mon Fertile finishing school in Switzerland – an aptly named establishment given that it was designed to prepare well-to-do young women for marriage and motherhood with a bit of housewifery and table-laying thrown in. She spent the summer term by Lake Geneva and the winter term skiing in Gstaad. The autumn term and spring term will have been spent learning how to walk – and seat a dinner party correctly, with the dowager duchess next to the Bishop. She also, as her friends of the time have recalled, lost weight, gained some cheekbones and learned how to kiss boys, a pastime she apparently described as 'quite deliciously wonderful'. Before returning to London, Camilla spent some time in Paris, where she would have learned how to French kiss too.

Camilla and Annabel, close, now they are both in their fifties, lending each other their bits of Alice Keppel heirloom jewellery for important parties, were two quite different sorts of girls in those schoolgirl and teenage days. As illustrated by the knicker-throwing disparity, Camilla was also the sister who was known for her showy behaviour with men, for being raunchy and randy. 'When a boy hove into view she could turn on the headlights – and how!' yelped someone who knew

Camilla, the debutante. People are fond of using these vehicular analogies – when Camilla and Charles first met an onlooker reported that they were like 'two steam trains heading towards each other at full pelt'.

During the school holidays Camilla would return to East Sussex and hang out with other teenage sons and daughters of the upper-middle classes – the hunting crowd, but also for a while, rather quaintly, the ballroom-dancing crowd. Richard Evans is someone who remembers going to ballroom dancing in 1964 in a church hall at Hassocks, a few miles away from Plumpton.

'Everybody had a chance to dance with everyone else. Camilla was there; and also we would have bumped into each other at the parties around Ditchling. The classes were held by Mrs Robinson. We went twice a week and we would invariably get asked back to someone's house. Camilla was always there.'

Plenty of fresh air, loads of animals, a bit of Enid Blyton, a bit of Jessica Mitford, some Sloane Square secretarial and a tinge of royalty – this is what made Camilla, what turned her into a bit of a blast, a 'gel' with spirit, a sexy roustabout who swore and smoked and was hearty – a girl from a poem written by her grandfather P. Morton Shand's good old friend, John Betjeman. She was a posh and horsey girl with big breasts and thank goodness for them: her bust size was, according to the spectacularly well-informed Broderick Munro Wilson, vitally important if she was to succeed with the opposite sex at that time, 'All our generation are breast men,' he said 'I can't go out with a flat-chested girl.'

Indeed Prince Charles once, quite rudely, plunged his hands into Camilla's cleavage at a party. He quite forgot himself and was apparently overcome with the very sight of it. Resistance was useless then, as it subsequently proved to be even within hours of his wedding to someone else.

'There was no one with more character,' said Munro Wilson of Camilla, 'she exuded self-confidence.' Or, as the cuckolded Diana put it back in 1995, 'If you look at pictures of her when she was younger, you can see she was a goodlooking woman... So why has she let herself go to pot?'

Chapter Five

If you look at the picture of Camilla that was taken by a *Harpers & Queen* photographer at her coming-out party on 25th March 1965, you can see that she was rather sweet-looking. Her skin is clear and downy. She's polished up nicely. Her hair shines and has clearly been 'done' – a bit of backcombing has gone on and she has a long fringe, a bit Joanna Lumley, that catches the light from the chandeliers at Searcy's, Pavilion Road, Knightsbridge, a popular party venue for girls whose London houses were a bit small and whose country houses were too remote.

Camilla looks gauche and timid, like a young girl who is wearing really grown-up clothes for the first time. She is standing next to her mother, Rosalind who has her Queen's hair-do and is wearing a pale silk-satin two-piece, three strands of pearls and one brooch. When Camilla joined the line-up of all the other debutantes that same year in order to curtsey to a big cake at Queen Charlotte's Ball, which is what they do, she, like all the other young 'virgins', wore white. But in a picture taken at her own party at the beginning of the 'season' – that four-month stretch between March and July during which upper-middle and upper class girls can meet boys they might like to marry – Camilla is wearing dark chiffon and a pair of very 1960s chandelier earrings. Her expression here is the one she has worn in most photographs since. She looks as if she might flinch if anyone makes a false move.

In fact, according to Jennifer – Betty Kenward, the *Harpers & Queen* social diarist, who wore her hair like the Queen Mother's but with a bow at the back – Camilla coped very well that evening, managing to mingle and fizz up a party atmosphere:

The Honourable Mrs Shand's cocktail party for her attractive debutante daughter, Camilla, was another successful party. This was one of the very first of the debutante cocktail parties and might have been a bit sticky as, at the beginning of any season, the young people have not yet got to know each other, but both the hostess and Camilla did plenty of introducing and it went with a swing.

Read this in the voice of Celia Johnson and you're there. The word 'attractive' is interesting. Jennifer/Betty was known for gushing a bit more than this; she could have said 'pretty', or 'lovely', or 'charming'. Describing Camilla as 'attractive' was like an estate agent saying 'versatile', or 'has character'. Which of course is what everyone did say about Camilla Shand. One debutante who was there observes, 'Camilla was never going to be Deb of the Year, but she was determined to have the best fun she could.'

Among the 150 or so guests that evening enjoying the best fun with Camilla were some friends who are still friends of hers now. Who they are and whom they went on to marry, have affairs with and in many cases divorce provides an early insight into quite how interwoven these people's lives are – how, in the world in which Camilla moves, the same world which inspires Jilly Cooper to write her sex and jodhpurs novels, the open marriage that Camilla went on to enjoy with

Andrew Parker Bowles was not unusual.

Take the Hon Kirsty Smallwood, for instance. In those days she was the Hon Kirsty Aitken, daughter of Sir Max Aitken. She is now married to Christopher Smallwood, the architect, but her first husband was Jake Morley who later married Davina Sheffield who used to go out with Prince Charles and whose first cousin is Angela Sheffield, a close friend of Camilla Parker Bowles who was also at Camilla's coming-out party on 25th March 1965. And there you have it: you may have run out of breath but you have achieved a Camilla Parker Bowles social circle.

Miranda Morley, Jake Morley's sister, was also at the party and she is still a close friend; as was Marilyn Wills, another close friend, who is the great niece of the late Queen Mother who was the grandmother of Prince Charles. There's another one.

Perhaps Camilla's closest friend of all, though, was Virginia Carington, known as 'Floribell' in her debutante days, daughter of the former Foreign Secretary, Lord Carrington (*sic* – the family name is spelt with one 'r', the barony with two), who went on to marry Camilla's uncle, Lord Ashcombe. (It didn't last.)

It was Lord Ashcombe who hosted a party for Annabel Shand at his country house, Denbies, outside Dorking in Surrey. Betty Kenward did not cover this event. In fact Annabel's was a very different sort of party altogether and it points up the differences between Camilla and her sister. Camilla's coming-out was the approved version, what the parents would have wanted, what a contemporary Mrs Bennett would have liked for her marriageable daughters. Camilla might have gone in for a little unsophisticated, Pony Club-style giggling and some slap and tickle behind the potted palms at Searcy's – her big earrings and a touch too much mascara might have nodded at the fact that it was 1965 – but Annabel's party was much more in keeping with the times, which were, as Bob Dylan was to put it so succinctly, 'a-changing'.

At Annabel's party an ambulance allegedly had to be called after one female guest who had never driven before crashed a car into Lord Ashcombe's stone gateposts. Dai Llewellyn (brother of Roddy who was Princess Margaret's boyfriend, and therefore very nearly Prince Charles's step-uncle) recalls passing a bottle of champagne to the car alongside him while driving home at 100mph over Putney

Bridge. According to Christopher Wilson in his brace of books, *The Windsor Knot* and *A Greater Love*, one young man never made the party: he was killed when he overturned his Triumph Vitesse on the Dorking bypass. 'It was the pre-breathalyser, last gasp of a pampered, aristocratic milieu which was about to be destroyed by the social changes set in motion during the 1960s.' Wilson also notes that most of these changes passed Camilla by.

Not all of them, though, because she certainly had boyfriends who she went to bed with, which was a very 1960s thing. Not just one boyfriend who she knew she was going to marry – which is the excuse girls gave for sex before marriage in the 1950s – but two or three boyfriends. The first one, according to Nigel Dempster, was a handsome nineteen-year-old called Kevin Burke.

Burke, son of Sir Aubrey Burke, the deputy chairman of the Hawker Siddeley Group, the aircraft manufacturers, and therefore very much the right kind of chap, never actually confirmed whether or not he went to bed with Camilla two days after her party as has been reported, but he has talked, really fondly and rather ruefully, about their time together.

'Every night we went to two or three cocktail parties and then a dance. All you needed was enough petrol for the car and to pay for your cleaning and the rest was provided. It was the best time, and I had the best partner you could wish for. She was never bad-tempered. She knew how to have fun. I remained with Camilla all that year. I suppose we were in love... as much in love as anyone can be at that age... Then she ditched me.'

Sounds like Kevin was really in love, and at that age you can be really in love so that it's terrible when someone ditches you. He seems to have forgiven her, though, maybe because she was 'like a big, boisterous puppy', and you forgive puppies when they leave dreadful messes behind them.

It wasn't Kevin Burke who described Camilla as a puppy but it was somebody who knew her at that time. It was someone who had been to the flat she shared with Virginia Carington at No 1 Stack House in Ebury Street. 'It was typical Camilla. Her bedroom looked like a bomb had hit it. Virginia was fairly tidy and organized and Camilla drove her nuts, in the nicest possibly way. Virginia once told me, "You know, Camilla has this inability to hang anything up on a hanger. And she has an aversion to cleaning fluids of any description.

You should see the state of the bathroom when she's been in it." But she was so sweet, it was impossible to be angry with her.'

Another friend, who was at the Searcy's coming-out party, recalls, 'She was one of the stars of the season. If you wanted a party to go with a swing, you invited Camilla. With Camilla around, you could guarantee the evening would never be dull.'

Soon after ditching Kevin Burke, Camilla went out for a while with Rupert Hambro, of the fantastically rich and powerful Hambro banking family. Then Andrew Parker Bowles hove into view; not so rich, not so powerful but dashed handsome and a bit aristocratic. Camilla turned her headlights on full beam.

Chapter Six

'Introduce me to him now.' This is what Camilla is reported to have said the first time she ever saw Andrew Parker Bowles at a party in 1966.

There are a few versions of this story. One says that she had gone to the party with Rupert Hambro and without qualms simply changed boyfriends during the course of the evening; she segued from one to the other like a horse changing legs in a show ring. She saw the handsome or 'almost beautiful', as someone has described him, Andrew Parker Bowles, and she was off.

Another version says that Camilla was with Simon Parker Bowles, Andrew's brother. Simon worked for Camilla's father at the Audley Street wine merchant's and he and Camilla were good friends who went about together. However it happened, from that night on, Camilla, when not at home in the country with the horses, could generally be found at her new boyfriend's flat in the Portobello Road.

'You would go around there on a Saturday morning,' recalls a friend, 'and Andrew would be up and about cooking breakfast and making coffee. Around eleven, Camilla would stagger downstairs looking bleary-eyed and a little dishevelled. She would walk around wearing one of his big shirts. She would sit on Andrew's knee and tease his hair. They clearly had a very lusty, healthy life together.'

A former girlfriend of Andrew Parker Bowles's has said 'his greatest gift to women was the knowledge that sexuality was healthy – something to be explored. That openness about sex was his gift to Camilla. She was very innocent when they met, but they spent many, many nights together. He schooled her in the ways of the world.'

Not all the ways of the world though. She might have had masses of sex, got up late and looked sexy and dishevelled in her boyfriend's shirts but there is no suggestion they did any of the other things young people did in the 1960s and early 1970s, like wear kaftans. They didn't wear flowers in their hair or take drugs or wallow around naked in mud at music festivals, or paint psychedelic daisies on their cars. From early on Andrew was serially unfaithful, so in his own way he was into free love, while Camilla, a girl in love, was more than willing to be true to her 'almost beautiful' soldier. Free love is what she, when she found out about his other girlfriends, and later the newspaper profiles called philandering. And Andrew Parker Bowles was very keen on philandering.

The same friend who witnessed the sexy, dishevelled Camilla on Andrew's knee told another insightful story which appears in Caroline Graham's 2001 biography, *Camilla, Her True Story*. She said that Andrew found it impossible to be faithful to Camilla and that he was particularly partial to the 'leggy Sloane Ranger type'. When Camilla wasn't around, he would pick these girls up at parties and take them back to the Notting Hill flat.

'One morning', says Caroline Graham's source, 'she turned up unexpectedly. Andrew opened the door dressed just in his underpants. For once he totally lost his cool. Camilla asked to be allowed in and Andrew started fumbling around for excuses. Camilla was livid. She said to him: "Who the hell have you got in there? Which tart was it last night?"'

Poor old Leggy Sloane, she never stood a chance as, 'red-cheeked', she attempted to fasten her bra-strap and pull her dress over her head at the same time. Camilla, having forced an entry, asked Andrew if he couldn't have done better than 'someone else's shop-soiled goods'. Then she made an about-turn and left. 'That was when Camilla decided that if she couldn't beat him, she would join him... She looked around for a while and then she found the biggest catch of all.'

It's completely riveting stuff and the minutiae are impressive, the red cheeks and the bra and the shop-soiled goods. It makes you wonder who told this story that it should filter down through the years and end up in such glorious detail in a biography 35 years later.

Was it a triumphant Camilla who told all her friends how she caught Andrew at it, or was it Andrew telling a raunchy anecdote, or was it poor Leggy Sloane who ended up in tears and then thought no more about it until she read in the papers that the shoe was now on the other foot, that Camilla had been playing away and as a result a royal marriage was on the rocks?

***

Camilla and Andrew were together on and off for seven years before they married. He was 27 and she was nineteen when they met. He was a lieutenant in the Blues and Royals, which was an amalgamation of his father's regiment, the Royal Horse Guards, and the First Royal Dragoons. He'd have gone to Eton if he hadn't been a Catholic. Instead he went to Ampleforth, then Sandhurst, then the Horse Guards. When Camilla was coming out in 1965 he was in New Zealand serving as an aide-de-camp to the Governor General.

So he was an army fellow like Camilla's father, he was horsey, an amateur jockey. The parents were excellent in-law material; his father, Derek Parker Bowles, was a best friend of the Queen Mother's, and was descended from the Earls of Macclesfield; he was a steward at Newbury racecourse, lived at lovely, big Donnington Castle House just outside Newbury – perfect. Through his father's friendship with the Queen Mother, the fourteen-year-old Andrew had been a page at the Queen's coronation, so his parents had an impressive picture to put in a silver frame on the piano in the drawing-room. A good egg, excellent company, a loyal friend, Derek Parker Bowles had once been well off. He had inherited a large amount of family property in Enfield in North London. But he was profligate, and by the time he died in 1977 there was very little left. He had lived off the capital all his life. A friend of the family says that Andrew 'was almost pulling up the floorboards to see if there was anything hidden'.

Andrew Parker Bowles's mother, Ann, whose nickname was 'Rhino', was Chief Commissioner of the Girl Guides, a sort of *über*-Brown Owl, and was made a Dame in 1977. They were right and proper people, four children, Andrew, Simon, Rick and Mary Anne, very keen on racing; Dame Ann's father was Sir Humphrey de Trafford, owner of the 1959 Epsom Derby winner, Parthia. And the cherry on the cake was that Andrew was so very good-looking. Camilla had scored. The Major and the Hon Mrs Parker Bowles, down in East Sussex, must have been pleased as summer punch.

***

'I certainly knew I wasn't the only person being

taken out by Andrew at the time,' said Lady Caroline Percy. 'There were always other girls... I never knew Camilla very well when we came out but if she saw I was with Andrew she would come up to me at parties and ask me what I was doing with her boyfriend. She was always doing this to girls at parties. But I got fed up with it and said to her, "You can have him back when I've finished with him..." Andrew behaved abominably to Camilla, but she was desperate to marry him. When I was with him I discovered he was also having an affair with a married woman.'

Every so often Andrew would be posted off somewhere for long periods of time. Once, when he came back on leave, he started seeing Princess Anne who was then nineteen and whom, royal watchers are keen to point out, he could never have married because he is Catholic. But this little dalliance, which included a four-day at Windsor Castle during Ascot Week in 1970, could well have been the crucial thing – the thing that sparked the whole Camilla and Charles affair off, the first domino. Because over the years Andrew kept on seeing Princess Anne. 'Many believe,' wrote Christopher Wilson, 'that it was to Andrew that she surrendered her virginity.'

Andrew was seeing other people too, but, as this particular theory, a theory that royal watchers are generally quite satisfied with, goes, the Princess Anne thing got to Camilla in a big way.

Camilla really, really, quite desperately wanted to marry Andrew Parker Bowles. She was in love with him and he was being difficult and elusive and playing the field which would have made a young girl feel wretched with love. This could well be why she chatted Prince Charles up one day at a polo match in the summer of 1970. He was a bigger royal with bigger prospects than Andrew's fling, Princess Anne. And while Charles may not have been as handsome as Andrew, he would have been looking pretty sweaty and macho post-chukka nonetheless. Polo and hunting are sexy pursuits – all that testosterone and all those glistening flanks.

Camilla wouldn't have been too fazed by him socially because she was among her own sort of people; the former debs with nothing much to do, who went to polo matches on summer weekends and whose parents, who knew the Queen, had nice houses in the country.

The precise first words that Camilla Rosemary Shand and Prince Charles Philip Arthur George ever said to each other are not known. It is unlikely if the two people involved remember what they said and if Prince Charles does, then he wasn't about to tell Jonathan Dimbleby, his biographer. Dimbleby gives the authorised version of their first meeting, which is that Charles and Camilla were introduced to each other by Lucia Santa Cruz, the daughter of the Chilean Ambassador. Lucia had met Charles when he was at Trinity College, Cambridge.

They were both guests at a dinner party given by Lord Butler, the former Tory minister and then Master of Trinity College, and his wife. Lord Butler had been consulted and briefed by the Queen and the Duke of Edinburgh and was, according to Jonathan Dimbleby, 'in an unrivalled position to ensure that the heir to the throne made the best possible use of his time at Cambridge'.

He and his wife, it transpired, were playing the Mountbatten game: Lucia Santa Cruz was picked out to be an early sex-motherer. As Mollie Butler wrote later in a memoir of her husband, Lucia was 'a happy example of someone on whom he [Prince Charles] could safely cut his teeth, if I may put it thus.'

Lady Butler was apparently most put out at suggestions that she was hinting in any way that the relationship might have been intimate, but it looks as if that is precisely what she was hinting at. What else could 'safely cut his teeth' possibly mean? In fact it doesn't look as if Charles had much teeth-cutting left to do. Luis Basualdo, a polo player, says that in those days when Charles spent weekends at the Basualdo residence in West Sussex they would all play 'Murder in the Dark' because it was Charles's favourite game. 'It meant getting close to the girls I had invited for him,' says Basualdo, 'Charles was self-conscious so it was also a way of avoiding chat-up lines. The girls hid in a darkened room. He'd find one and start kissing her. He would lead her to a sofa or a bed and have sex with her, there and then. He had four or five farmers' daughters and the girl from the butcher's shop.'

Just as thrilling but perhaps a teensy bit less 'Carry On' is the unauthorised biographer Caroline Graham's account of how Camilla and Charles finally met:

The rain lashed down and gusting winds whipped across the polo fields at Windsor Great Park.

Prince Charles, his hair slicked down by rain, was standing beside one of his beloved polo ponies, stroking the animal's damp mane. Suddenly, a lone figure dressed in green wellington boots, brown corduroy trousers and a dripping wet green Barbour jacket appeared by his side.

'That's a fine animal, Sir,' said the woman.

Turning around, Charles found himself looking at the woman who was to dominate his life for the next quarter of a century.

With a relaxed smile, she said: 'My name is Camilla Shand. Very pleased to meet you.' *But she didn't say that very non u*

This is the version they should use when they make the mini-series.

So Camilla seduced the Prince, they were famously photographed under a tree at a polo match that summer looking absorbed in each other, like sad and serious young lovers. They saw each other whenever he wasn't off with the Royal Navy. She also saw Andrew Parker Bowles whenever he wasn't off with the Blues and Royals and Andrew Parker Bowles also saw Princess Anne who was shortly to meet Mark Phillips, causing Andrew to propose to Camilla.

The sorts of people we are dealing with here

were summed up by one who said, at the time of Princess Anne's divorce from Mark Phillips in 1992, 'The trouble with Mark was that he was from an inferior regiment and came from an inferior background to Andrew, so we all knew it wouldn't last.' They were snobs – rank and upbringing counted for more than fidelity or loving, lasting marriages.

It didn't really matter at that stage whether Camilla loved Charles or not because she could only ever have seen him as a temporary measure. She was really very determined to marry Andrew Parker Bowles. No matter how much she liked the Goons, how well she knew the words to 'Ying Tong Tiddle I Po', no matter how much she and Charles both loved their horses and their dogs, and, despite the Alice Keppel connection, she could never have seriously believed an affair based purely on historical symmetry could last very long.

But it must have been an exciting novelty, suddenly being in with the Royals, weekends at Broadlands, dinner at the palace, playing at family with the Queen. As one friend of Camilla's explains it now, 'You have to remember that practically everything he says to her is going to be interesting. If he is telling you about something that has happened with his mother and his mother is the Queen then it automatically becomes quite, quite fascinating. Camilla has a ringside seat. I think that is what she likes, having the ringside seat. She knows the truth, and wouldn't we all love to really know the truth? And then sometimes you can spill little bits of the beans and that in turn makes you interesting.'

Prince Charles, on the other hand, was in love with Camilla. He'd seen in her what all those other people had seen, all those school chums and co-debs who said she was no great shakes in the looks department but she was tremendous fun, a character, someone with spirit, a great companion. 'Pretty, bubbly, and she smiled with her eyes as well as her mouth. Unlike some others he had met, she lacked coquetry and did not preen herself. She laughed easily and at the same sillinesses that brought him to tears of laughter,' wrote Jonathan Dimbleby.

There is no doubt, Charles was smitten. But as he told Dimbleby, he wondered who on earth would take him on. '...To accept his hand in marriage would be to enter a contract as much with an institution as an individual and to accept obligations that would go far beyond the conjugal bonds imposed either by the Law or by the Church. His consort would be the future queen, the object of insatiable curiosity, and the creature of public whim.'

Public whim was, even in those days, guided by the press and, fortunately for her, the press had yet to get a whiff of Camilla. They were looking in the wrong direction, sniffing around the leggy Sloanes, Anna Wallace, Sabrina Guinness, Davina Sheffield, Lady Jane Wellesley, Lady Sarah Spencer. They didn't see Camilla and the Prince skulking behind that tree. And they still hadn't caught on completely when, twenty years later, Andrew Morton to all intents and purposes ghost-wrote the Princess of Wales's autobiography, which told us there were more than two people in that marriage and exactly who the third person was.

Chapter Seven

In much the same way that nobody really knows what their first words to each other were, nobody really knows exactly when Camilla and Charles became lovers. It might have been the night he went back to her flat in Cundy Street after they had been to Annabel's nightclub in Berkeley Square together. Princess Anne was at the nightclub, too, without Andrew Parker Bowles, because he was in Germany being an adjutant. Christopher Wilson writes perceptively that Prince Charles and Camilla 'danced to the hits of the day, Eric Clapton's "Layla", the Bee Gees' "Run to Me", Michael Jackson's "Ain't No Sunshine", Roxy Music's "Virginia Plain", and when things slowed down Charles and Camilla took to the floor for Python Lee Jackson's "In a Broken

Dream" and Faron Young's "It's Four in the Morning".

And, Wilson concludes neatly, at four in the morning Charles and Camilla were in her ground floor flat, 'discovering a passion which was to last many long years; years of joy and sometimes of adversity, but years where never once would the love die'.

It might not have died, but it wasn't strong enough on her part to stop Camilla from marrying Andrew Parker Bowles in June 1973.

'I suppose the feeling of emptiness will pass eventually,' wrote Prince Charles to Mountbatten after hearing about Camilla's engagement. He was a sad and lovelorn fellow, emotionally and physically marooned in Her Majesty's navy wondering what had happened to the 'blissful, peaceful and mutually happy relationship' with the big-bosomed Goons fan he had left behind in London.

'His father sent him to sea in a boat for nine months,' Munro Wilson said, 'What do you do?' What Prince Charles did was wake up one morning and find that his two-timing girlfriend was going to marry her Barbara Cartland hero, her soldier not her sailor.

'You immediately become geographically undesirable,' said Munro Wilson as if that explained everything, which it didn't. What is more likely is that Camilla knew that she and Prince Charles would never have married even if they had been allowed to because what she wanted was her handsome, outgoing, bounding, heart-throb, not her forlorn, introverted Prince who needed cheering up all the time with whoopee cushions and Spike Milligan impersonations.

Camilla and Andrew were married in the Guards Chapel in Birdcage Walk on 4th July 1973. It was a big society wedding: assorted godchildren, nephews, nieces and cousins made up the sixteen bridesmaids and pages and there were so many guests that 300 extra chairs had to be found for the chapel.

Andrew Parker Bowles was recovering from a stag night at White's club where everyone got drunk and broke the glasses and plates. His old girlfriend, Princess Anne, was a guest at the wedding the next day. The Queen Mother was there and Princess Margaret came along for the wedding breakfast at St James's Palace. This concentration of royalty in one place at the same time, along with some pretty swanky titles, caused the event to be described as 'The wedding of the year', in the society magazines. Poor, bereft Prince Charles, meanwhile, was floating around the West Indies on a frigate.

Camilla does not look great in her wedding pictures. Those who question Mrs Parker Bowles's hair-style should take note. Don't knock the fringe – she needs the fringe. On her wedding day she had it scraped back into her veil. It was a look that really wasn't working for her. Still, the veil was sprinkled with jewels and one guest commented that the bride sparkled as much as the diamonds she wore – the girl who laughed with her eyes as well as her mouth, whose inner something shone through. Andrew looks handsome, heroic and happy.

They spent their honeymoon in the South of France and then moved into a house in Wiltshire called Bolehyde Manor where they set about recreating a version of their parents' houses – probably a bit shabbier given the differences between floppy-fringed Camilla and twin-set Rosalind.

In the 1970s people like Camilla didn't move in and start hiring interior designers. They knew exactly what to do with their comfortable sofas, tapestry cushions, pretty rugs, inherited bits of 18th-century furniture and ancestors in gilt frames. They didn't need an interior designer, who would at any rate only have been an old unmarried schoolfriend with an eye for colour and proportion, to tell them where to scatter their cushions.

Camilla would just know that you put the pheasants – wedding-present silver pheasants – in the Pledge-scented dining-room and the Herend china rabbits in the alcoves either side of the fireplace in the drawing-room. The commemorative enamelled boxes from Halcyon Days in Brook Street which would be added to each year by your godparents would be put next to the silver-framed wedding photos on a round table next to the sofa.

The downstairs loo had the husband's army commission in a frame as well as some larky photos taken during the courtship; her sitting on his knee, twirling his hair around her finger, wearing his shirt, and another of the groom with watery eyes and his bowtie askew, raising a glass at the stag night. These were joined a few years later by more photos of their children, on ponies or playing in rock pools and a wet spaniel shaking, just out of the water. The kitchen had the Aga and the dog baskets, which were lined with threadbare towels.

These days Robert Kime, whom Camilla later

hired to re-do the post-Diana Highgrove and who became so close to Charles and Camilla he even went on holiday with them – he also went on to redo Clarence House after the Queen Mother died – does for his clients pretty much what Camilla did innately back in 1973 at Bolehyde, but without the plastic Addis bin in the kitchen. And today the dog baskets would be covered in a pink and blue rose print from Cath Kidston.

Nigel Dempster describes Bolehyde manor as a 'splendid mansion'. In fact it was a very big country house, with lots of bedrooms for weekend house parties and some paddocks for the horses – just the job.

Camilla was 26 and as fine as she could be. She had done what she was supposed to do. She didn't have any qualifications to speak of and that in itself was a qualification for someone who was set on a life of gymkhana committee meetings and pruning, nothing too academic to cloud the quite considerable amount of common sense required to fill in an entry form, load up a horse-box and drive across the county in time for a handy hunter competition.

Camilla had survived the 1960s, apparently without the help of any psychedelic drugs and without throwing her knickers too far afield, and she had her lovely, cigaretty, ginny life stretching before her. She might have got bored. But she didn't. Andrew may well have been away from Monday to Friday, he commuted to and from London on a weekly basis, now a major in the Blues and Royals, and he may not have been faithful – he almost certainly wasn't – but Camilla always had Charles. And if he wasn't physically with her they had the long-drawn-out 'Night, night my darling, I don't want to put the phone down,' phone calls. She always, always had the one she called 'My favourite little Prince'. He needed his sex-motherer too much not to have come sniffing around her marriage.

In fact, immediately after the wedding, he wasn't physically around much because he was in the Navy. The rumours which surfaced in the early 1990s, in the wake of Camillagate and Andrew Morton, that the Prince is Tom Parker Bowles's father, are not true. But that is not to say that Charles and Camilla weren't having an affair. They were. Maybe he did try to fall out of love with Camilla during those years when he was photographed playing around in the sea with Tahitian lovelies who draped him in lotus blossom. He certainly put himself about a bit.

A former courtier once pondered what it was that had spoiled the Prince, 'And I've come to the conclusion that, after he'd had such an awful time at Gordonstoun, he suddenly found himself in a world where everybody, and the ladies in particular, had their arms wide open. Instead of the world being at his throat, it was at his feet. Of course, it was easy for him to attract women. He only had to raise an eyebrow or flick a finger, and almost anyone he fancied would oblige. Modest women, some of them married, fell like ninepins, and you'd have needed to have been jolly strong-minded not to go to bed with women who threw themselves at you like that.'

There were others on whom he appears to have had hand-wringing, apologetic, puppy-love crushes, when he behaved more like the shy and gentle child he had been – the kind of child, said Lady Mountbatten, 'who if he had two sweets, would always offer you one'.

There was Janet Jenkins, for example, a receptionist at the British consulate in Montreal where he paid an official visit. He met her at a cocktail party in 1975, when Camilla would have been preoccupied with her six-month-old baby son Tom, and he met her again in 1976 when he went back to Canada to watch Princess Anne ride in the Olympics. He wrote to Janet and the tone is the same over-courteous, clumsy-old-me one he used in his letters to Earl Mountbatten and later in the Camillagate phone conversation.

'I don't know what you think but if you could bear to see me…'; and in another letter, 'I was so looking forward to the possibility of seeing you but I tried hard to restrain my optimistic sentiments in case all my hopes were to be dashed, and dashed they were.'

Not to worry. Lovely warm Camilla was there in her kitchen, with her dogs and her Aga, ladling out some nice, sweet mothering. Nobody seemed to mind about her and Charles and certainly nobody in those Pre-Diana/Morton days was telling.

Even when Andrew was at home the Prince would sometimes be there too. Visitors have described him sitting patiently like a small, cold child in the kitchen waiting for Camilla to see her guests off after a dinner-party. He wouldn't join the others at table because it would have caused an atmosphere and in those very early days the trusty inner circle had yet to be established – someone could have gossiped. Sometimes Prince Charles would slope off upstairs to the nursery with something nursery-ish, shepherd's pie or macaroni cheese on a tray. He was like the Winslow Boy, arriving home unexpectedly out of the rain, wanting nanny to give him a hot bath, a milky drink and, in the Prince's case, a quick dip into her cleavage.

And Andrew, it seems, was all for it. He is, wrote Nigel Dempster, a man of 'reserve' and 'phlegm'. One old hunting chum went as far as to say that, 'He loved every second of it. The idea is to keep it in the family. Better us than them, you see.'

In other words, it was all right if it was royalty or aristocracy – it didn't matter then. If Camilla was going to compete with her husband in the adultery stakes then that was fine as long as it was the Royal Adultery Stakes, or at the very least the People Like Us Adultery Stakes. What they didn't want was a Lady Chatterley situation – no game-keepers, gardeners or grooms – it was fine as long as it was among their own kind. Andrew Parker Bowles was thus able to behave in such a way that led another soldier to describe him as 'from a bygone age – an old-fashioned soldier for whom honour is everything. He embodies all the old virtues that people used to stand for; that the Royal Family used to stand for, really. You always looked up to them once. You can genuinely look up to him now. He is that decent.'

Being decent, of course, also kept the heat off him – and his philandering. If Camilla hadn't had her Prince, would she have minded Andrew's infidelities? 'The Parker Bowleses had a very English marriage,' said a family friend. You just bite the bullet and keep going. Camilla was terribly loyal... He would have had the ladies, and she would have had a nice joint of beef on the table and nice things for the children. That generation had a whole different code. Nobody ratted on anybody else.'

Well, actually, Lord Charteris did. He told the Queen that her son was sleeping with the wife of a brother officer in the Brigade of Guards, 'and the regiment doesn't like it.' 'There was a drawback,' said one former member of the Royal Household. 'We were warned never to include Mrs Parker Bowles in the guest list for any formal event where the Queen was to be present.'

'It spoke volumes,' said another insider, 'that she did nothing further about her son sleeping with a married woman. If she had taken a stronger line, maybe things might have been different.'

Three decades later a marvellously gossipy account of an early Charles and Camilla meeting was to emerge. It came to light in the wake of Jonathan Dimbleby's authorised biography of the Prince, the biography that failed to acknowledge that anything adulterous had ever happened before the Prince's own marriage to Lady Diana Spencer had 'irretrievably broken down'.

An unnamed butler who worked for Camilla's grandmother, Sonia Cubitt, at her house, Hall Place in Hampshire, emerged from the woodwork and told this story about the recently married, new mother Camilla and the bachelor Prince Charles. 'I well remember the first time the Prince came to Hall Place. He arrived at 6pm and after a few minutes talking to Mrs Cubitt he vanished into thin air with Camilla.

'She had been wandering around all day wearing a pair of jeans with no zip – the flies were held together with a safety-pin. This sort of behaviour shocked Mrs Cubitt and she demanded to know whether Camilla was going to change into a frock before the Prince's arrival. "I can even see your drawers, Camilla," I heard her bellow. Camilla's reply was, "Oh Charles won't mind about that." The manner of her reply indicated that it didn't matter because he'd seen it all anyway.'

Then there was the story about the worried detective looking for the Prince who had gone missing in the gardens at Hall Place which Christopher Wilson recounts in his book, 'I told him not to worry,' said the anonymous butler, 'they were taking a stroll, and I persuaded him not to go looking. He'd have been very embarrassed if he had – they were up against a tree doing what Lady Chatterley enjoyed best. I saw it myself. As soon as they went into the garden they headed straight for the avenue of beech trees and into the shadows – they were oblivious to everything around them.'

And if it hadn't been Prince Charles, it could well, even in those early years of her marriage to Andrew, have been someone else – possibly someone else's husband. And the wife who was cheated upon could well have been a friend of Camilla's and would in all likelihood have remained a friend of Camilla's while having an affair with Camilla's husband herself. As one writer once put it, the behaviour of this particular set harked back to a time when 'the great country houses had nameplates on the bedroom doors to guide nocturnal adulterers to their destinations'.

Having extra-marital sex is something they did – not all the time but occasionally, as you would occasionally go salmon fishing or point-to-pointing. As Camilla's friend Jilly Cooper put it, 'I'm sure every county is the same. I bet Worcestershire is just as degenerate. Horses always lead to these things. Horse-boxes with straw, people not knowing where you are, the availability of alibis. Also, a helicopter is a very good aid to adultery.'

That Camilla was unfaithful to her husband didn't make her a bad person. She may not have balked at breaking her wedding vow, but she was still 'nice', in fact she was 'jolly nice'. She was a 'jolly nice girl', with loads of friends, a husband whom she fancied rotten, two children who loved her for her gameness and lack of pretension, and a third child in the shape of a Prince who couldn't cope without her.

And so Charles and Camilla and Andrew bumbled along together through the 1970s, with three in the marriage, sometimes four if Andrew was flush in the filly department. Laura, Camilla's second child, was born in 1978, and while it was known that the Prince of Wales was a good 'friend of the family' – he was Tom's godfather – there was, miraculously, no further scandal leaking from that strong band of friends. Nobody was scandalised by the fact of Camilla and Charles until Lady Diana Spencer entered the picture, and even then those who knew it for a fact didn't seem to see that there was a problem.

***

It is hard to reconcile Camilla, the woman who vetted the sacrificial girl bride, with the 'jolly nice' Camilla. And she did vet Diana. She vetted all the queen contenders. Anna Wallace, a girlfriend of the Prince in 1979-80, knew that she was being vetted by Camilla. The question is, did she and the others know what they were being vetted for? Was it their potential as a royal bride she was assessing, or was she gauging how much of a threat they might be to her own arrangement with Charles?

At a polo ball at Stowell Park, Lord Vestey's estate in Gloucestershire, Prince Charles, who was supposed to be with Anna Wallace, headed straight for Camilla and stayed with her for the rest of the evening. Anna Wallace wasn't hanging around to watch. She borrowed a car and drove herself home. At the Queen Mother's 80th birthday party at Windsor, she told him 'I've never been treated so badly in my life. No one treats me like that, not even you.'

So Camilla looks like a two-timing schemer, a sizer-up, a procurer of young, marriageable aristocratic girls who, if they do not pass muster will be relegated to the reject pile. She does not look at all the cosy motherer, or the good, laid-back mother of Tom and Laura. When Tom Parker Bowles became restaurant critic for *Tatler* magazine in 2001, he gave an interview to Nigel Slater the cookery writer. He said 'Mum does the best roast chicken in the world. Sometimes it's roast lamb. Mum doesn't go in for puddings much, but we have the best Sunday roasts.'

This is good Camilla, putting the roast beef on the table, taking a break from her needy Prince, King Whinge, as he is known in Gloucestershire, retreating to her own house and her own 'blood family', to borrow a phrase used so emotively at Diana's funeral.

She probably roasted Diana a few chickens, before giving Charles the go-ahead. In Diana, she saw a young, sweet, meek girl who wouldn't hurt a mouse. In fact, she said, she was a mouse. That is how Camilla described the young woman who in a few short traumatic years would grow up and call her a Rottweiler: she said she was a mouse.

And so he proposed. Nobody knows if Prince Charles ever had any real intention of being faithful to his wife. He told Jonathan Dimbleby that after his engagement to Diana he only saw Camilla once and that was four months later – to say farewell. The famous 'Gladys and Fred' bracelet (Gladys and Fred are their Goonish nicknames for each other, although Charles told Dimbleby that his nickname for the great love of his life was Girl Friday) was bought, the Prince said, on the advice of one his friends. It was intended as a gesture to Camilla to prevent her feeling as if she had been dumped by the Prince now that he was engaged to the peachy, young one, and it was Michael Colborne, his personal secretary, who was sent off to buy the bracelet.

Prince Charles also told Jonathan Dimbleby, famously, during the interview he gave as part of an ITV documentary, broadcast in 1994, that he didn't commit adultery until 1986, after five years, when his marriage had 'irretrievably broken down'. Perhaps he simply did what he was told – Prince Phillip had instructed that he should 'Give the marriage five years; then, if it is not working out, look elsewhere.' Nigel Evans, the editor of *Majesty* magazine posited that Prince Charles was just sticking to the job description, 'Having a mistress is more of a job requirement than anything else.'

In February 1981, though, when he became engaged to Lady Diana Spencer, Prince Charles wrote in his diary, 'I expect it will be the right thing in the end.'

'I thought that he was very much in love with me,' said Diana to Morton, 'which he was, but he always had a sort of besotted look about him, looking back at it, but it wasn't the genuine sort.'

Chapter Eight

In a photograph taken of Camilla and Diana in 1980, as the vetting procedure would have been coming to its spectacularly wrong conclusion, the two of them are pictured, huddled together around the paddock at Ludlow races. They are both watching Prince Charles, who is about to ride in the Clun handicap for amateur riders, and they look rather surreptitious, as if they are colluding about something, talking about him, maybe teasing him behind his back. Although it is around this time that the story of Charles and Camilla divides into two camps – the 'Of course he stopped seeing Camilla' camp and the 'He had no intention of being faithful to Diana' camp – we now know that, whatever Prince Charles's resolve, it is Diana who is being colluded against by the woman who is pretending to be her friend. In the picture Camilla is biting her thumb anxiously, she is looking pretty sneaky.

There is no evidence that she ever actually liked Diana when she took her under her wing and had her to stay in the country so she could make her assessment and then tutor her in the fickle ways of the Prince ('I'd been staying at Bolehyde with the Parker Bowleses an awful lot,' said Diana, 'and I couldn't understand why she kept saying to me, "Don't push him into doing this, don't do that." She knew so much about what he was doing privately and about what we were doing privately... if we were going to stay at Broadlands... I couldn't understand it.') – but perhaps Camilla saw in this sparkling but shy young thing similarities to Queen Alexandra who so stoically tolerated Mrs Keppel.

It is unlikely that she ever regarded Diana as a friend, a mate, a confidante. As one intimate recalls, Camilla said, 'The good thing about Diana is that she will love him a lot.' Love is something which most mothers take for granted in their children's marriages – except Camilla, we mustn't forget, wasn't actually his mother and she rather glaringly failed to say how much she hoped Diana would be loved by him. This could well be Camilla's real strength – why her relationship with Prince Charles has lasted as long as it has – she only ever thinks of him. She would never have used the phrase 'even by you', as Anna Wallace did, she would never say, 'Not even you can behave like this.'

Camilla doesn't come out of this part of the story well. Up until now she is likeable. She is strong, hearty and wholesome and loyal and she has that inner something that made her peers at school call her 'Milla' and want to be her friend.

But now she looks like a villain, a cackling, conspiring Cruella de Vil. Even her tight band of friends would have difficulty defending her now. So instead they fibbed or closed ranks and, regardless of what they might have said amongst themselves, they never for a minute publicly blamed either her or him.

'He was the loneliest man on earth, and he was landed with this lovely but slightly idiotic child,' said one of them, the implication being that what happened was out of anyone's hands, especially Charles's wringing hands. Quite who it was who had landed him with the idiotic child is not specified. Was it the Queen Mother, whose best friend was Diana's grandmother, Lady Fermoy? Was it Prince Phillip, or was it simply that Diana did a very good job of duping the right royal lot of them and thereby landed herself on him and England?

If that was the case she still can't really be blamed. Most nineteen-year-olds can be pretty idiotic. She was being herself and if that meant being meek and starry-eyed in front of a royal Prince then she was no different from any other girl her age, no matter how many royal connections, or sisters who had been Charles's girlfriend she had; no matter how many childhood summer holiday afternoons she might have spent around a swimming-pool with the young Princes Edward and Andrew.

Camilla, meanwhile, was to all intents and purposes working on behalf of her favourite little Prince, serving her country, finding us a Queen. Unfortunately for everyone, she, along with the Queen Mother and Lady Fermoy, lobbied for the wrong one. Diana was wrong for the Prince.

Several of Charles's friends were horrified at his choice. Three of them – Nicholas Soames and Lord and Lady Romsey, Mountbatten's grandson and his wife – warned him that he was making a big mistake. Penny Romsey, according to Jonathan

Dimbleby, sensed an absence of intensity in the Prince's feelings for Diana and thought that although Diana had fallen in love, it was with the idea of being Princess of Wales rather than the man. Penny Romsey told her husband Norton Romsey how worried she was and later, on a ride through the park at Broadlands, the estate he inherited from his grandfather, Norton argued her case strenuously with Charles but, writes Dimbleby, 'succeeded merely in provoking the Prince to an outburst of indignation'.

By this stage Camilla would have wanted the whole wretched business sorted; and afterwards there was the promise of a return to her lovely life with the trug basket and the county set and if the Prince came to call then she'd be there for him with a nursery supper and a consoling laugh at his weak jokes.

She can't have meant Diana's marriage to fail (although she might have secretly hoped that there would be room for a third person). She's not a bad person; she just got Diana wrong.

And so Charles proposed; the engagement was announced and the blundering, clumsy Prince made that stupid remark, 'Whatever love means.' Camilla must have wanted to give him a good slap.

He could have given the game away with that. The country, as represented by a normally hyper-cynical press – a press which could, like an interfering prospective mother-in-law, only be looking for trouble – was in fact in an unusually romantic mood and the bunting and street parties were quite defiantly in the name of happily ever after. Prince Charles could have ruined all that. And it really wouldn't have hurt him to pretend.

And so, from then on, they were very careful. And it wasn't that difficult because everyone was so obsessed with Diana – 40 or 50 photographers outside her flat every day – nobody thought to keep an eye on Charles. So that when Camilla sneaked on to the royal train while it sat in sidings in Gloucestershire one evening, for a pre-wedding tryst – perhaps, to give them the benefit of the doubt, even a farewell tryst – everyone thought it must have been, impatient, love-stricken, infatuated Diana slipping through the shadows. There was a bit of tut-tutting over the young lovers who couldn't wait until their wedding night but that was all; nobody suspected, and for eleven years Camilla and Charles got away with it. But Diana knew it wasn't her. Diana knew, even while she clung to the satin and roses picture in her head, the dreams that had been fuelled by the pink and powdery novels of her step-grandmother, Barbara Cartland. Those dreams were, it turned out, all she had, and she was going to cling on to them for dear life. She wanted to be the royal princess with a royal prince who really loved her; she wanted to be the one the slipper fitted.

Charles took the time to write to friends to tell them how lucky he was that 'someone as special Diana seems to love me so much' but he never told her, or us, that he loved her back. He thought her special presumably because she was young and soft and apparently without guile. She was special as in unusual because, unlike 'come up and see me' Camilla, who laughed with her eyes and wore her boyfriend's shirts, Diana was a virgin.

This, of course, was a prerequisite. Other required qualities read like an advert in the back of *Horse and Hound*: gentle nature, good with children, doesn't kick out, bomb-proof. Camilla gave Diana the once over, passed her fit and, before Diana knew where she was, her face, as her sisters so prosaically put it, was on the tea towels. Twelve years later James Whitaker, the *Daily Mirror*'s royal correspondent, and Nigel Dempster both went to America to promote their books about the crumbled royal marriage. Whitaker said Camilla had spent the night with Prince Charles just 36 hours before his wedding. Dempster said this was rubbish but did acknowledge that Charles had tried to break the engagement off. 'The point about the royal children is that they don't have a mother, they have a monarch,' said Dempster. And the monarch said the show must go on.

At the ball which was held in Windsor Castle on the eve of the wedding (the Prince danced once with Diana and several times with Camilla), Charles told a friend, 'I believe I'll have a marriage like that of my grandmother and King George VI. That was an arranged marriage but became one of the most loving ever. Diana and I will grow together just as they did, through shared duty and children.'

The problem was that he had no intention of beginning that growing-together process until after the wedding. He was too busy worrying about Camilla to bother about bonding with Diana. He failed to phone Diana when she went to Australia for three weeks after his marriage proposal. She had gone away with her mother to – as Diana put it in the tapes she made for Andrew Morton – 'sort of settle down and to organise lists and things... ' He sent her flowers when she got back, but didn't think to write a note to go with them.

During the run-up to the wedding, Charles made touching, loving gestures in the direction of Camilla, like buying her the Gladys and Fred bracelet. Meanwhile, his 'special' young fiancée complained to her friends that she had been left to fend for herself in the big scary palace.

When Diana was told to move to Clarence House the evening before the announcement of the engagement, Camilla already knew. So she was able to leave a note – dated two days previously – on Diana's bed asking her to lunch. And now she really does look like the manipulative other woman. She didn't have to put the date on but in doing so she was sending a message to Diana, proving that she was right in there with the Prince, that they were like two peas in a pod, that she, Camilla, knew exactly what was going on. This was psychological warfare. 'Such exciting news about the engagement,' wrote the wicked mistress. 'Do let's have lunch when the Prince of Wales goes to Australia and New Zealand. He's going to be away for three weeks. I'd love to see the ring, lots of love, Camilla.'

'So I organized lunch,' said Diana, 'we had lunch and… very tricky indeed. She said, "You are not going to hunt are you?… You are not going to hunt when you go and live at Highgrove are you?" I said, "No." She said, "I just wanted to know."'

Camilla was just checking that they could still meet on the hunting field – covertly meeting in a covert. Charles apparently loves to watch Camilla in full flight with the Beaufort hunt. One member describes her as a ruthless horsewoman, aggressive, shouting in the hunting field. Someone else said, 'You should hear her screaming as she approaches a fence. She'll be shouting, "Bloody hell. Get out of the fucking way!"'

Camilla's life up until now had neatly dovetailed the Prince's life. They hunted together and he could get a nice frisson out of watching her. They fished together during country-house weekends. They went to the same dinner-parties, and shared the same circle of friends. They could do this because Camilla and Andrew had their arrangement. Camilla was, for the purposes of her relationship with Prince Charles, a free agent. But suddenly Charles wasn't. He had no such arrangement with the wistful virgin bride he was about to marry who was being watched by the whole world.

Everyone was looking. He couldn't be too careful.

As Diana walked down the aisle of St Paul's Cathedral with Charles, she imagined her new husband looking for his mistress. She told Andrew Morton, 'I spotted Camilla, pale grey, veiled pill-box hat, saw it all, her son Tom standing on a chair. To this day you know – vivid memory.' Why did Camilla wear grey? Perhaps it was the next best thing to black and she wanted Prince Charles to see she was in mourning. As far as Diana was concerned, she might as well have worn shocking pink, stood on the chair herself and shouted, 'Cooo-eee!'

Patty Palmer-Tomkinson believes that what Prince Charles wanted from Diana was: 'Love, support, loyalty and a real family life – which is something he never had.' When the marriage failed, Charles's friends were outraged at suggestions that he'd married her as a brood mare. 'The reason why he didn't marry until he was 30 was precisely because he didn't want a wife simply for that reason. If he'd wanted nothing but a brood mare there were any number of girls willing to fulfil that role for him. He just wanted a normal, lifelong, happy marriage.'

Chapter Nine

After Diana's death, Andrew Morton was free to admit that the Princess of Wales had contributed to his book via tapes she had originally made, rather curiously, for a voice coach called Peter Settelen, who later, showing spectacularly few scruples, appears to have cashed in handsomely by selling them to the American television network, NBC. In Morton's updated version of the book, which included transcripts of these tapes, he wrote that she was so anxious not to be seen as paranoid or foolish that she produced several letters and postcards from Mrs Parker Bowles to Prince Charles to prove that she was not imagining their relationship.

'These billets-doux,' wrote Morton, 'were passionate, loving and full of suppressed longing...'

Prince Charles kept these letters in the drawer of a dressing-table in the master bedroom at Highgrove, which, given that he had entire palaces in which to hide them, makes you wonder if perhaps deep down he wanted them to be found.

Diana once overheard Charles on the phone to Camilla. He was in the bath and he told her 'Whatever happens, I will always love you.'

'We had a filthy row,' Diana told Morton.

At home Charles lived with tantrums and tears; a bulimic wife who later admitted that she was obsessed with Camilla and that she dreamt about Camilla at night. With Mrs Parker Bowles, on the other hand, Charles had that suppressed longing luring him back to the Aga and the ample bosom. Back to the woman who didn't feel, like most wives do at the end of a long day, that she had to match him woe for woe, compete over who was the most worn out. Camilla would just listen and, if she did moan, it was in harmony with him, it was on his behalf; she moaned for his work load, his family who didn't understand him, and, most of all, for the marriage in which he was trapped.

'Camilla never passed judgment,' said a friend, 'she was never particularly nasty about Diana. She was just a great, great friend who would listen for hours and never get bored.'

Perhaps Prince Charles did try to make his marriage work and did try to give Camilla up. But he didn't grow to love Diana, as George VI grew to love his bride. Instead they grew to hate the sight of each other. His best, if that is what he gave, wasn't good enough; it was woefully inadequate. Every so often he lost control and, if Diana called him names and threw things, he would call her names and throw things. He once gripped a bathroom basin so tight that his knuckles turned white and then, fired with rage, like the incredible hulk, he ripped it from the wall.

If it had just been the Princess's eating disorder he had to deal with, a pretty big deal in itself – if all he had had to do was guide her gently, with his hand in the small of her back, into royal life, be her mentor, be a fatherly husband – then perhaps he could have coped. It is unlikely. But he would have stood a better chance if he hadn't also had to deal with a wife who was convinced, rightly or wrongly, that he was having an affair.

At the heart of all Diana's problems was Camilla and the Prince couldn't actually, truthfully deny his Camilla. To deny her would have been to betray her. She was real, Diana wasn't making her up, she existed right there in that marriage. She was Rebecca to Diana's Mrs de Winter, only Rebecca was dead and gone, a bad memory, an undiscovered corpse at the bottom of the sea. Camilla was there, living and breathing and ruining everything because Charles loved her and not his wife.

It was only the press who hadn't discovered her and even when Diana told them about her via Andrew Morton, still those reporters and royal watchers didn't quite have the nerve to say it was true. Many royal reporter stalwarts wrote that Diana had got it wrong, that Camilla was no more than a confidante, a bosom friend, and that every man, especially a stressed-out prince, has a right to a bosom friend.

A member of the Charles camp, the Highgrove set, a Camilla denier, recalled, 'I think Diana believed that he must be communicating with Camilla, because if he didn't love her he had to be seeing someone else. The whole world adored her – Diana – so why didn't he? She couldn't compete with it, because it wasn't there to fight. It was a phantom. I think she almost invented it as a rival. By going on about the rival so much, Diana gave Charles no reason not to go back to the rival.'

Even if this is true, even if Camilla wasn't physically seeing Prince Charles in those early days, she was there in Diana's head and in her dreams and she was certainly there on the end of the phone, a refuge for him from the storms Diana whipped up. As the Princess told Andrew Morton, whenever she found new evidence of Camilla – a letter, a cufflink, an overheard phone call – there would be 'rage, rage!'

Camilla was in her face. Camilla, Diana thought, was the reason they lived at Highgrove which was only eleven miles from her house, and she was probably right. Highgrove, which was bought by the Prince in June 1980, a year before his marriage, was bricks-and-mortar evidence of the colluding, the fact that she had been duped. It was also near to many other friends of Prince Charles's, which only served to widen the chasm between Diana and her disco-hating, fogey husband. Diana's friends and Charles's friends were rarely mutual ones. In 1986, when the Parker Bowleses moved from Bolehyde Manor to Middlewick House in Corsham, Wiltshire, and Diana went with Charles to the house-warming, she would have been struggling to make county small talk with his closest allies. And when the party was over and they returned home to Highgrove they would have one of their set-piece confrontations about Camilla, and Diana would have told Charles he didn't understand her and that she didn't want to talk about architecture or Laurens van der Post, and that Scotland might be beautiful but it was cold and wet and there weren't any clothes shops and why couldn't he even try and like Dire Straits, and then he would have stormed off and phoned Camilla and around and around they would go. Diana would then take the children and the nannies and her 'rocks' – the policemen who watched her – back to Kensington Palace, change into something Lycra, head off to the Harbour Club for a work-out and Charles would have himself smuggled to Camilla in the back of a Vauxhall Carlton Estate driven by his policeman. Back to Camilla's unconditional mother love.

Among friends they were quite open about the nature of their relationship, and sometimes they forgot that they weren't only among friends – that there might be people watching who were tell-tales. Some years after the event, a story surfaced about a polo club ball, which both Charles and Camilla attended. Andrew was there and he along with everyone else watched while Camilla and Charles kissed like lovers – French kisses. Andrew commented, 'HRH seems to be awfully fond of my wife and she seems to be fond of him.' He didn't seem to think it was too much of a problem.

But mostly they were all too careful. When royal engagements caused the Prince to travel around the country, or it just wasn't safe to be with Camilla at Middlewick or Highgrove, there were the safe houses, Charles and Camilla's very own Travelodges, the big country homes belonging to that tight circle of friends, the ones who tapped the sides of their noses and said, 'Mum's the word.'

First up is Dummer Grange in Hampshire, TPT Towers, the home of Patty and Charles Palmer-Tomkinson. Charles and Camilla were safe as houses here. They would also stay with the Duke and Duchess of Devonshire at Chatsworth in Derbyshire, and at Eaton Lodge on the Duke of Westminster's estate in Cheshire. This safe house is owned by Anne, Duchess of Westminster, widow of the second Duke. Charles stayed here after hunting in 1989 and it was from here that, exhausted at the end of a busy week, missing his comforter who would have been with him if only someone had organized his diary better, he made the Camillagate phone call.

During that conversation, incidentally, Camilla mulled and moaned and mentioned Garrowby Hall at Pocklington, near York, as a possible hidey-hole, the home of Ernie, the Earl of Halifax. Ernie is married to another Camilla, Camilla Younger of the beer family, and she was once married to Andrew Parker Bowles's brother Rick, so there is another one of those Camilla social circles – people who knew other people who were once married to someone who is related to Camilla. And they were all in on the secret which they kept because Charles was the heir to the throne and, poor fellow, he had a terrible life and Camilla was a jolly nice girl who understood him and was therefore serving her country.

Also brimming with poignancy and nostalgia is Broadlands. Charles and Camilla stayed here together in the early 1970s, before Camilla married Andrew Parker Bowles, at a time when the house belonged to Prince Charles's beloved uncle, Louis Mountbatten. This is also where Diana spent her hopeful honeymoon night. Broadlands now belongs to Earl Mountbatten's grandson Norton and his wife Penny. When their six-year-old daughter died of leukemia in 1991, Diana cried hard at her memorial service. Her tears were for the dead child but she was also distraught to see Camilla in the congregation. 'Diana was upset,' wrote Andrew Morton, 'that Camilla Parker Bowles, who had only known the Romseys for a short time, was also present at such an intimate family service.'

In fact Camilla probably felt she had every right to be there. She, the Romseys, their extended Mountbatten and Knatchbull families and even their house went back a long way and one, probably apocryphal, anecdote which has trickled down through the years since the early 1970s places Camilla right in amongst the Mountbatten family. Camilla (Shand, as she was then) was having lunch one day with the bachelor Prince Charles at Broadlands, where she, fulfilling her early sex-motherer role, would often spend weekends with him as he fulfilled his young Prince-who-has-to-sow-his-wild-oats-before-finding-the-virgin-bride role. They would sleep together in the Portico Room where Charles and Diana, the only 'girl of sweet character' the Prince could in the end find to marry him, were later to spend their wedding night. Above the bed hung an 18th-century print of a beauty at her toilette with a suitor at her feet and the accompanying verse '*Egards, tendresse, soins, tout s'épuisse en ce jour. Bientôt, l'Hymen languit et voit s'enfuir l'amour*' – 'Consideration, tenderness, courtesy, all flows from this day. Soon Hymen [the god of marriage] will languish and behold, love will fly away.'

At the beginning of lunch on this weekend when Camilla stayed, along with several other members of the Romsey family, Camilla began stroking a Labrador under the table and then she got on with her soup. A few minutes later, feeling a wet nose nudge against her knee, she put her hand down again to stroke the Labrador. But this time there was no Labrador. Her hand reached blindly, and in vain. The dog had vanished and when Camilla told everyone at the table what had happened there were gasps of surprise and disbelief because there could never have been a Labrador at all. The Labrador had died a few days earlier.

Whether or not this story is founded in any truth whatsoever it is still interesting for what it says about Camilla – raunchy and game and a bit of a sex-pot she might be but she is also thought to be the sort of comfortable, earthy person to whom a spectral Labrador (as well as a needy Prince) might head.

***

The Camillagate tape tells us that by the late 1980s Camilla and Charles were used to spending Sunday nights together. By this time Diana and Charles had separated in all but name.

'It's like that programme "Start the Week". I can't start the week without you,' said Camilla, in her long, drowsy, sexy drawl. Wherever they were, wherever they slept together, official royal engagements permitting, was where Camilla would start her week – with a drive back to Wiltshire in time to walk the dogs, have a snack lunch, do a spot of gardening, feet up on the sofa with a stiff gin, and wait for the next call from Charles to tell her how really ghastly and appalling his day had been since she left him. And she would say, 'Oh darling. I wish there was something I could do, I would do anything for you, perhaps I could come over to Highgrove on Thursday.' And he would tell a select number of policemen and aides to expect her and she would tootle through the lanes to Highgrove.

She lived her lovely dog-hair-and-horses life: her children who were away at school sometimes came home on exeats or for holidays, Andrew was sometimes home and the Prince was sometimes at his home just up the road which is when she would jump in the car and set off for a bout of cushion-plumping.

In 1995 Ken Stronach, a senior aide to Prince Charles for fifteen years, a key Camilla facilitator, betrayed them both and told his story to the *News of the World*. He said that on the Prince's bedside table was a rosary, given to Charles by the Pope during a visit to the Vatican with Diana in April 1985. There was also a brass lamp in case of power cuts and a candle in a holder. And then there was a phone, a special unbuggable phone, for calling Camilla and Her Majesty the Queen on and a small, enamelled box with the Welsh dragon on it in which he kept the cufflinks Camilla had given him with the entwined 'C's – the ones he couldn't resist wearing on his honeymoon. Later, in 1994, after a robbery at St James's when some of Charles's belongings were stolen, including supposedly, the cufflinks, the press office said the cufflinks had never existed. Diana must have dreamed them up – it was like *Gaslight* – poor, deluded Diana. One senior aide said: 'The story of the Camilla cufflinks is simply a myth – there weren't any. But we took the view when the story emerged that His Royal Highness should not stoop to deny such fictional tittle-tattle.'

But, most importantly of all for the purposes of analysing their affair, on that table next to Charles's bed there was a photograph in a walnut frame of Camilla smiling into the sunshine on a garden bench outside Birkhall, the Queen Mother's house in Scotland which has since been bequeathed to Charles.

Opinion is divided over whether the Queen Mother was complicit in Charles's affair with Camilla. Whether the nation's favourite smiley granny, setting a fine example, bowling along through the Blitz, buckling down and doing her duty, came to condone her grandson committing such flagrant adultery. She had loathed Wallis Simpson for luring a king from his throne – so why wasn't she worried about Camilla?

Possibly it was because Camilla was the daughter-in-law of one her closest friends, Derek Parker Bowles, and because the Queen Mother was very keen on horseracing and a stiff gin and tonic herself – although Camilla's favourite drink is a manhattan. Perhaps the Queen Mother had little sympathy with that difficult, high-maintenance trouble-maker Diana whom she regarded as someone who should have done what she did – put up and shut up.

Or could it simply have been that Camilla Parker Bowles was staying at Birkhall with her husband Andrew when that photo in the walnut frame was taken? Camilla and Andrew stayed with the Queen Mother every year. The Queen Mother was very keen on game old Andrew Parker Bowles, a former amateur jockey who once completed the Grand National on his own horse, a member of the Jockey Club and chairman of Sandown Park, a steward at Cheltenham and Newbury. He would escort the Queen Mother to Sandown and the Cheltenham Festival every year. She would invite him to stay with her at Royal Lodge, Windsor, to go racing with her there and he would stay with her every summer at Birkhall. And Camilla went too, and so did Charles and if, by the by, Camilla and Charles were tiptoeing mischievously like Sid James and Barbara Windsor along corridors in the middle of the night, then Andrew probably was too, and if he wasn't then it was only because an opportunity hadn't presented itself.

***

Ken Stronach's tittle-tattle provided some pretty scurrilous royal minutiae – that Charles would meet Camilla in the garden at Highgrove while Diana slept and return with grass stains and mud on his pyjamas. 'There was muck and mud everywhere,' Stronach reported, 'They had obviously been doing something in the open air.'

When Diana was away, Stronach was less busy with pyjama maintenance because the indiscretions were committed inside, in the dry. But this arrangement wasn't ideal either as it gave Stronach just as much of a headache on the security front. Camilla would be given a guest bedroom and Charles would switch off the security systems that protected his own room so that she might nip along in her nightie, and visit him. 'It was a big risk,' sighed poor, worried Stronach, 'but he's blind to everything where the lady is concerned.'

'The lady' would be woken, by Stronach, in the morning and would return to her own room. If this last unlikely detail is true, it gives a really terrible insight into this affair; two grown-up people who have to be told when it is time to get up in case the journalists find out they have slept together – like two small children being woken by nanny in time to brush their hair and clean their teeth before breakfast. Why couldn't they have woken themselves up with an alarm clock? Why couldn't they tell the staff to take the morning off? Perhaps Charles really is incapable of squeezing his own toothpaste – a tasty morsel of gossip which seeped out after the Paul Burrell trial in 2003. He could always have asked Camilla to do it for him, it wouldn't have been any trouble because she'd do anything for her favourite little Prince. Stronach also said that the staff at Highgrove were told to treat Camilla as if she was the mistress of the house. She would sit at the top of the table at inner circle dinner parties and pretend to be the hostess. 'It was as if the Princess never existed.'

Another piece of gossip from a former servant emerged in 2003, when Paul Burrell, Diana's 'rock', published his biography. One night, instead of retiring early as Diana had believed, Prince Charles had sneaked out from Highgrove to see Camilla.

When Diana had then phoned Highgrove and asked, 'I don't suppose the hubby's around is he?' Burrell had replied, 'I don't know, your Royal Highness.'

'Of course you do, Paul. You know everything that happens down there. Now, where has he gone?'

'The best person to ask would be His Royal Highness,' said Burrell, 'not me.' But Diana got the information out of him in the end and Burrell went to bed 'worried sick'. The following day Prince Charles asked him, with pursed lips, 'Can you tell me why Her Royal Highness is constantly aware of who visits or phones Highgrove when she isn't here?' He asked him when he had last spoken to Diana.

'His face was puce red,' wrote Burrell, 'and he bellowed "Why?" ...Puce turned to virtual purple ... he picked up a book from his table and hurled it in my direction. I can still see the fluttering pages whirring through the air. It missed, but I don't think it was intended to hit me.' Burrell ends this account with an hilarious quote from Prince Charles, 'I am the Prince of Wales,' he yelled stamping his feet, 'and will be king!'

Diana and Charles rarely went out socially together – an invitation sent to both of them was usually only meant for one of them. And when Annabel Goldsmith hosted a birthday party for Camilla's sister, Annabel Elliot, she really did not expect Diana to turn up. But at the last minute Diana announced that she would go and it was on this night that, after finding Camilla and Charles and another male guest chatting together in a downstairs room, she confronted her husband's mistress.

Diana told Andrew Morton, 'I thought, "Right, this is your moment," and joined in the conversation as if we were all best friends. And the other man said, "I think we ought to go upstairs now." So we stood up, and I said, "Camilla, I'd love to have a word with you if it's possible," and she looked really uncomfortable and put her head down, and I said to the men, "Boys, I'm just going to have a quick word with Camilla."' The Princess told Mrs Parker Bowles that she wasn't 'born yesterday' and she knew what was going on. She said she was sorry that she was in the way, and that she knew it must be hell for both of them. She didn't say how Camilla reacted.

Chapter Ten

1992 was the year the Queen called her *annus horribilis* and, to be honest, it wasn't a great year for Prince Charles or Camilla Parker Bowles either, or for that matter for Andrew Parker Bowles. It wasn't a great year for Diana or even the Duke and Duchess of York, or Princess Anne. 1992 was the year of: *Diana, Her True Story* by Andrew Morton; Squidgygate, an inane bugged conversation between Princess Diana and her friend James Gilbey; Princess Anne's divorce from Captain Mark Phillips; and the Duchess of York's toe-sucking interlude with her financial advisor in Italy.

And then Windsor Castle catches fire; and then, as if that wasn't enough, finally – the icing on the cake – in December the Prime Minister,

John Major, announces that Charles and Diana are separating.

It is hard to imagine all that happening in one year. All these incidents seem, in hindsight, isolated by their sheer bloody awfulness. And then came Camillagate in early 1993, and Prince Charles told a friend that he dreamed of living in Tuscany and that he sometimes considered giving the whole king business a miss.

The first dire thing to happen in 1992 was the lonely Princess in front of the Taj Mahal photo opportunity – a gift to the press pack who weren't remotely bothered about the Indian royal tour or its purpose: the £1.5-billion arms deal it was intended to promote. They were only concerned, quite understandably given that it was beginning to look as if we were all being hoodwinked, with the state of the Waleses' marriage. There she stood, the forlorn wife, colourfully but balefully on her own, wearing rainbow red and purple, while grey, unromantic Prince Charles gave a speech to the Indo-British Industrialists' Forum.

Two days later, with all the dramatic emphasis of an auditioning *Dynasty* starlet, Diana turned away from Charles as he attempted a peck on the cheek after a polo match. It was an official peck on the check, not a spontaneous one. The days of spontaneous pecks were over. The Princess had been coerced into handing out prizes to members of the winning team, and Charles had no choice but to line up and take his turn with all the other players. 'The Princess moved her head almost imperceptibly to the side, leaving his kiss to die in the air,' wrote Jonathan Dimbleby. Prince Charles doesn't have much luck with his trips to India; eleven years later, in October 2003, he went on his own, not even with Camilla to cause controversy, and while he was gone Paul Burrell published his autobiography and at the same time a former servant made some really scurrilous, probably untrue allegations. Prince Charles entered one of those periods in his life from which it looked as if he would never recover. There were a few of these to come.

Next up in the *annus horribilis* was the Andrew Morton book. In 1987 Morton, then a royal reporter on the *Daily Star,* had written a short, prescient article, 'Separate breakfasts, separate timetables, separate friends. These days the Prince and Princess of Wales are leading active, interest-ing, but totally different lives.' Five years later Morton expanded on this and wrote a long, interesting book that was serialized in the *Sunday Times*. And one of the most important people in this book was Camilla Parker Bowles, for it was she, Morton wrote, who Diana dreamed about. It was Camilla who, according to Morton/Diana, had caused the Waleses' marriage to fail, caused the bulimia and the suicide attempts.

Not everyone believed this – the Camilla deniers rallied round their dear friends, the Prince and Mrs Parker Bowles, and, two years later, in his 1994 biography, Jonathan Dimbleby, a vehement Camilla denier (even Camillagate makes no more than a footnote in his book), wrote: 'Certainly she [Diana] was unable to acknowledge what their friends and especially those who were close to Camilla Parker Bowles knew to be the truth, that the relationship [with Camilla] had ceased entirely, as the Prince had relayed to her before they were married.' He went on to say that the Princess seemed unable to rid herself of a further suspicion that the Prince and his friends were conspiring to deceive her, that they were in some 'unfathomable' way against her.

What the Prince's conspiring friends conspired to say in the wake of the Morton book was, 'He [the Prince] wants all of us to say nothing and nothing is what we will say.' The press, meanwhile, were prowling around Camilla's house in Wiltshire, although there seems to have been an element of confusion about where she actually, physically, was. Some say she 'vanished' but hung around long enough to be asked about the book – 'I haven't read it,' she said, 'but I will with interest when the time comes.' Another version is that she was trapped inside under house arrest – they said spikily that she was experiencing a little of what Diana had been forced to put up with.

Andrew Parker Bowles, for his part, said of Morton's revelations, 'It's fiction, fiction. I have nothing to say.'

Both he and his wife were most definitely out and about, though, on the day that the *Sunday Times* serialization began, at Windsor Great Park, watching polo in the Royal Enclosure, invited by the Queen.

Camilla, rather bravely and gamely, wore a Prince of Wales check suit although a friend, when asked about the significance of this, answered that it was probably the only clean outfit in the scatty old thing's wardrobe. Dear Camilla may not have been very tidy or smart or kept her clothes clean but she was, they said, a really nice human being who was being put unnecessarily through the mill by that neurotic nincompoop Diana.

Jilly Cooper was there at the polo that day and she flung her arms around her friend and told her 'You must not be sad.' She did sterling stuff with the press, too, telling a *Daily Mail* reporter that Camilla was 'a wonderful woman', who was coping bravely with the situation. 'This is hurting Camilla and her family very much. She is a lovely person with a great sense of humour and she doesn't deserve to be unhappy. Both she and Andrew have... spent ages laughing at the reports in the newspapers. It is really awful to see her being crucified like this, but I'm sure she'll come through it OK.'

Jilly Cooper had good reason to think that humour would play a part in Camilla's psychological survival. She did seem to laugh her way through many of these indignities and tortures and calumnies, as the Prince described them. Earlier in the year, when returning from a holiday in Italy with her friends Emilie van Cutsem and Amanda Ward, she was recognized by other passengers on the aeroplane, and she adopted a comedic 'Allo Allo' accent whenever a member of the cabin crew spoke to her and snorted and smirked like Milla who had snuck out on the school roof for a cigarette.

Meanwhile, on that June day, while his mistress watched polo with the Queen at Windsor, Charles, the reason for all the fuss and hullaballoo, was at another polo match altogether – at Cowdray Park, where his team lost 10-7.

And still they, the royals, kept rolling along. While all this was happening, while all the Morton/Diana revelations were being analysed and pored over, the Prince and Princess of Wales attended a ceremony for the Order of the Garter together, at St George's Chapel, Windsor. They also rode down the royal mile together in a carriage to Royal Ascot. Diana was snubbed by Prince Phillip in the royal box when she got there but it was nothing compared to what happened to Andrew Parker Bowles.

'Andrew Parker Bowles was admiring the fillies being paraded before him at Ascot,' writes Caroline Graham in her book, *Camilla, Her True Story*. It could be that Graham knew absolutely that the race about to be run was the Queen Mary, a race for two-year-old fillies. Or it could be that she hadn't a clue which race Parker Bowles was about to watch, but simply chose to use the word fillies because fillies can also mean pretty women and Parker Bowles likes pretty women.

Up until this point, post-Morton, any discussion of Andrew Parker Bowles's wife's affair had been behind his back, but today, as Graham relates, the Brigadier heard someone calling out to him. 'Ernest Simpson! Hey, Ernest Simpson! Why don't you come over here?' It was The Duke of Marlborough's younger brother, Lord Charles Spencer-Churchill, and Andrew wasn't having it. He may have tolerated, even condoned Camilla's affair, not being one to call the kettle black, but he was blessed well not about to be compared to poor simpering Ernest Simpson, in the paddock at Royal Ascot, with some of his best chums, including the good old Queen Mum, watching.

'He calmly turned around to face Churchill,' writes Graham. ' "Come over here," he commanded. A rather shaky Churchill lurched across the paddock. Andrew grasped him by the arm and thrust his face towards him. "I don't ever want to hear you talk to me again like that, do you hear? NEVER!" ' Spencer-Churchill later told Nigel Dempster that Parker Bowles was 'very, very angry indeed. He pummelled my right arm and shoulder extremely hard. The next day I was black and blue with bruises. I thought it was just a tease, a bit of a giggle. But Andrew didn't find it amusing at all.'

A few months later, Lord Soames, an old friend of Andrew's and the father of Charlotte Hambro, an old girlfriend, quipped that Parker Bowles was 'so loyal to the Crown that he is prepared to lay down his wife for the sake of his country' and it is unlikely that Andrew found this desperately funny either.

A married couple, Joan and Robert Wakeham, freelance husband-and-wife paparazzi, were, during this time, also making Andrew and Camilla's lives difficult. They took and sold pictures of the Parker Bowleses with their children in the gardens of Middlewick house. When Camilla or Andrew arrived home late at night, the Wakehams would run ahead of the car, up the drive, with Robert Wakeham screaming, 'Get the bastard!' On one occasion, Andrew Parker Bowles pinned Wakeham against a wall and called him a 'miserable little worm'. The Wakehams were nicknamed the 'Wackos' by royal detectives.

In June 1992, on top of everything else, Camilla suffered a financial hitch because she was a Name at Lloyds and she lost approximately £15,000. It wasn't enough to change her comfy life in any way but it isn't hard to imagine her performing a Basil Fawlty-esque series of sarcastic thankyous to God. She was receiving hate-mail in the wake of the Morton book and, to escape it, she went to Wales for a few days to stay with her former brother-in-law, a very close friend of both hers and Charles, Nick Paravicini – a provider of a safe house and a vehement Camilla denier. In November 1992, after the Morton book and just two months before Camillagate, Paravicini said, 'Andrew says his wife has never slept with Charles and I believe him.' That's how good a friend he was.

However, in 1996 a former housekeeper of Paravicini's told the *Daily Mirror* that Charles and Camilla had been regular guests at the house since 1992, that they stayed there often. 'They feel safe here because nobody knows about the place. She's quite snooty, you know. Quite grand, and she doesn't tip. And I'm not terribly keen on her habits. After she's been staying, I find knickers all over the place.' It was very unusual, at this stage, while she was still the secret mistress, for Camilla to be described as snooty or grand and perhaps she thought that if Charles could get away with not tipping so could she. A close friend, one who

143

does acknowledge that Camilla has her faults, some even quite substantial ones, and that she is in no way a saint, says, 'She is quite mean. I once bumped into her coming out of the dry cleaners and she was in quite a lather about how much it had cost her to have a dress cleaned. "Seven and Six!" she said. She was outraged.'

Others disagree that she is grand or difficult. Diana might have called her the Rottweiler but the staff at Highgrove thought of Camilla more, someone said, 'as a pussycat or a wet spaniel'. A friend of hers says, 'She is very clever about not casting any atmosphere about her. You don't worry about going up to her, thinking it might be presumptuous, as you might if it was Princess Anne or someone. Charles is surrounded by people who have that atmosphere but Camilla is completely un-neurotic.' If Camilla did leave her underwear lying around, then, and expected other people to pick up after her, it would have been because of her tendency towards scatty, dormitory untidiness that her friends talk of so warmly.

The *Daily Mail* columnist Lynda Lee Potter wrote that she suspected 'Camilla possesses an aristocratic arrogance which makes her indifferent to other people's feelings.' And Julie Burchill

Above left: The Shand girls with their mops of curls, 1952. Above right: Camilla in 1965 at her 'Coming Out' party with her mother, Rosalind. Left: The girl who laughed with her eyes (at a ball in 1983).

Top: Polo — a sexy pursuit. Above: Camilla marries her soldier in 1973. Opposite: The vetting procedure — Camilla escorts Diana to watch Charles riding at Ludlow races in 1980.

Above left: Prince of Wales check – Camilla with her family
at a polo match in the wake of the Andrew Morton serialisation.
Below left: Indignities, tortures and calumnies – paparazzi
photographs of Camilla in her swimming costume, tied to the gates
of Kensington Palace. Above: The second 'Coming Out' – at the
Ritz Hotel in January 1999.

Above: Camilla with her children, Tom and Laura. Right: With her father, Major Bruce Shand, after a service of remembrance at Westminster in 1992. Bottom right: Ray Mill House, in Wiltshire, just a 20-minute drive from Highgrove. Above right: Snow Queen – hunting is their passion.

She Loves the Life... Above: with Elton John

wrote, in her book *Diana*, 'When all is said and done it is a story about one woman [Camilla] hurting another over a long period of time, without having the soul or the imagination to put herself in the other woman's shoes.'

Both women are probably right and only women could have written so viciously about another woman. But Camilla is not a woman's woman. She is a tomboy who likes being one of the lads. She loves men, she is fond of her loyal band of girlfriends, but she prefers men. She is not a softie. No one says, as they said of Diana, that she goes out of her way to help people or comfort them, that she writes thankyou letters immediately or sends presents. But they do say that she cheers people up just by being herself, bounces them along with that inner something – she is good old, bad old, Tigger-ish Camilla.

And the same friend who says she is mean – or as he also puts it, 'she shares a sense of frugality with Charles' – says, too: 'Camilla isn't bad, but perhaps she is unfeeling.' Except of course towards the Prince. She feels very deeply for the Prince.

Their friend Patty Palmer-Tomkinson said, 'Camilla rings me from the car when the photographers are chasing her, and she tells us all the dreadful things that have happened, but she never tells the Prince of Wales. Camilla says, "Please don't let him know about this, he'll be so upset and worried." And I say I can't bear his not knowing, and she says, "Please don't." It's completely unselfish – maybe the way one loves a child.'

Shortly after the Paravicini visit, Camilla went on a brief holiday to Venice. She stayed at the Cipriani with her parents and her sister. Charles and Diana, meanwhile, were sent off, like errant children with a clip round their ears, on a second honeymoon that fooled no one. Diana topped up her tan, Charles moored himself at the opposite end of John Latsis's yacht with his friends who were also Camilla's friends but not Diana's friends. Diana said he spent most of the time on the phone to Camilla.

A former aide of Prince Charles's told a newspaper that even at this stage, with all the marriage-gone-bad rumours bouncing off newsdesks, Charles would take tremendous risks to be with or talk to Camilla. It was said that on Friday afternoons, as he drove from London to Highgrove, Charles would instruct his protection officers, who until then had been following his Aston

Martin up the M4, to leave him at junction 17. Then he would career off, like a freed horse into a field, to Camilla's house, and only one protection officer was allowed to follow him and that officer would sometimes sit outside Camilla's house throughout the night. The press would later enthusiastically describe these visits as romantic trysts and that is precisely what they were. Even though, by Dimbleby's reckoning, Camilla and Charles's affair had been going on for five years, and by others' calculations a lot longer, their encounters, because they were snatched, must have been hectic and romantic and they were definitely trysts. A Highgrove estate worker described how Charles would sometimes travel to Camilla's place incognito by commandeering a filthy Ford for the journey. 'I remember talking to a friend over at Middlewick and they told me the first time the car appeared in the driveway they were contemplating towing it away because it was so filthy.'

***

The horrible year seeped on into that summer of 1992 with Squidgygate, which many people saw as Diana's comeuppance, although this taped conversation – which included that memorable, marvellous phrase, 'after all I have done for that fucking family' – was, it turned out, nothing compared to the James Hewitt gossip which took another two years to surface. And neither was it as humiliating as the photographs of the Duchess of York's bit of hanky-panky with John Bryan in front of the little York Princesses.

But the royal road show still continued rolling on regardless and in August, for the sake of appearances, the Prince and Princess of Wales went on their final tour together, to Korea. They scowled their way through it; it came and went, and the newspapers continued to speculate that the marriage was over.

In October, Major Shand attended a memorial service in Westminster Abbey for those who had died during the Second World War battle at El Alamein 50 years before. Shand had fought in the battle and had intended to go to the memorial service with his wife Rosalind, but she was too ill and frail, so Camilla went with him instead.

A *Daily Mail* report doesn't describe the service itself, but does devote 1,000-odd words to the 'Two women in the life of Prince Charles...' coming face to face. 'They were like the twin faces of war – the dullness of defeat and the radiance of victory. As a piece of theatre it was compelling... If yesterday was a battle between these two women, there was no question that Diana was the winner.' The article describes Diana with eyes wide, bright and open, wearing a jacket of shimmering silvery grey and a tight-fitting white skirt.

Camilla by contrast was a funereal figure – pale, thin, hair flecked with grey, in shapeless, sombre blue as she 'shuffled' out of the Abbey. 'Was this indeed Diana's day of triumph?' asked the *Mail*, failing rather to remember the reason for the memorial service. 'It was very good of her [Camilla] to accompany me and she couldn't have been better company,' said Major Shand. 'But I think she found it a bit off-putting to be confronted by 30-odd photographers outside Westminster Abbey.' He was asked about his daughter's health and he said, 'As far as I am concerned, she is very well and remains in good spirits. The constant press scrutiny does not seem to have taken its toll on her.'

Still, it was clear that poor Camilla could do nothing right. In November she went to a Windsor ball in a taffeta ballgown and was described by the *Evening Standard* as wearing a Land-Rover of a dress. She had probably had it for years: it was the dress she wore for going to balls – simple as that.

Also, in November, rumours of the existence of a tape-recorded telephone conversation, in which Charles allegedly told Camilla he loved her and adored her, started to appear in the newspapers.

Charles, trapped in his painful marriage and describing Camilla as the light at the end of a 'rather appalling tunnel', must have told her he loved and adored her thousands of times, so the bugged telephone call could feasibly have been any one that he had made to her in the last decade. A friend of Camilla says, 'I was struck when she stayed with me, how often he rang her up. It would have driven me mad, if anyone rang me up like that. You are either driven mad or you love it and she obviously loved that sort of dependence on her.'

Charles and Camilla would have known, would have been told which phone call it was and that the tape, which had already been dubbed Camillagate, contained the excruciatingly embarrassing conversation in which the Prince had imagined being reincarnated as one of Camilla's tampons. As a denouement to this terrible year it was a right cracker, and all they could do was sit and wait for someone somewhere in the world to publish and damn them.

Andrew Parker Bowles dismissed the rumours as 'absolute rubbish', and Major Shand said, 'My family stand united. Camilla can compete with this.'

Charles and Camilla will not have been consoled by the fact that more than anything else the Camillagate tape was a testament to how very real and deep their devotion to each other was. It revealed two emotionally tortured people who, despite everything, should perhaps just be left alone to be together. But it would be several years before that would happen and for now the royal family and the Parker Bowleses were still mired in the *annus horribilis*.

On 9th December 1992 John Major made his House of Commons statement – 'It is announced from Buckingham Palace that, with regret, the Prince and Princess of Wales have decided to separate.'

Camilla was once again put under house arrest by the media and, when asked to comment, she said, 'Obviously, if something has gone wrong I'm very sorry for them. But I know nothing more than the average person in the street. I only know what

I have seen on television.' The first part of this statement may well have come from the heart. Camilla is not someone who wishes ill on other people. She may not have liked Diana but she didn't set out to hurt her. As her friend said, she is not bad. The second part of what she said, however, was clearly dishonest. Camilla knew a great deal more than the average person in the street. She knew that the marriage to the mouse, who, as it turned out, was capable of roaring spectacularly loudly, had been over before it had ever really begun and that she, Camilla, had had a lot to do with it.

Camilla gave this quote on her way out of Middlewick. She was with her sister and they were on their way to a very nearby safe house – Bowood House, the home of their dear, reliable friends, the Shelburnes.

Chapter Eleven

The Camillagate tape is a recording of a private phone call between Prince Charles and Camilla Parker Bowles which took place on 18th December 1989. It was one of three royal conversations recorded by an unknown snoop during a three-week period around new year 1990 and subsequently leaked to the media. The others – one between the Duke and Duchess of York and one between the Duke of Edinburgh and an anonymous woman – were not published, presumably because there was nothing remotely scandalous about the Duke of York talking to his ex-wife and nothing remotely interesting in the Duke of Edinburgh's rumbly growlings to another member of the aristocracy, and if he did say anything politically incorrect it would hardly have been news – it's what Prince Phillip does.

The Camillagate tape fitted all the right criteria, though, and it was first published in the second week of January 1993 by an Australian women's magazine called *New Idea*. The *Sun* newspaper which published in the same week was the first paper to do so in the UK. Others followed. The editor of the *Daily Sport* said he expected his paper's circulation to double to more than 400,000 as a result of publishing the transcript. 'We increased our print run by 20 per cent and we expect to sell every copy,' he said.

Norman Lamont, the then Chancellor of the Exchequer, denounced the publication of it in any paper anywhere. Meanwhile little spats erupted here and there. *Kent Today,* which printed the transcript in full, argued rather eccentrically on their front page that their readers had a right to know what 'this threat to our peculiar way of life actually is'. Roger Gale, MP for North Thanet, got involved, saying that while he appreciated that this was a relatively new newspaper seeking to establish itself, he was 'deeply saddened'.

Auberon Waugh, when asked if he thought the Camillagate transcript should have been published, said 'They seem quite a sporting pair. Only the gutter press should publish it, and everyone else should pretend not to have read it.'

While bigger, more resounding opinions were expressed – in the government, the Church, the palace – hundreds, possibly thousands, of these little 'was it right or wrong to publish'? confrontations went on all around the world. And there were smaller, but more meaningful, personal consequences, too. Poor Tom Parker Bowles was forced to listen to other boys at his school reading the creepiest sections of the transcript out loud in mock Charles-and-Camilla voices.

Camillagate was published in France, Germany, Spain, Italy, Portugal, Greece, the United States, Canada, South Africa, Zimbabwe, India and Brazil. In Greenwich Village, a New York theatre company laid on a production called 'Loose Lips' in which the Tampax section was acted out and in Italy they were calling Charles 'Prince Tampaccino'.

On the day of the Camillagate phone call, Prince Charles had been in Wales, visiting a youth enterprise centre, an old people's home and a technology park – which goes some way to explain how frustrated he sounds on the tape. He had finished up at Anne, Duchess of

Westminster's house, Eaton Lodge in Cheshire; and, before going to sleep that night, he had phoned his lady love.

The recording began a couple of minutes into the conversation, which is a shame because we miss hearing how they greet each other on the phone: 'Hello, it's me,' 'Hi,' 'Hello my darling.' Probably the latter; there are 23 'darlings' throughout.

Charles: He was a bit anxious actually

Camilla: Was he?

Charles: He thought he might have gone too far.

Camilla: Ah well.

Charles: Anyway, you know that's the sort of thing one has to beware of. And sort of feel one's way along with – if you know what I mean.

Camilla: Mmmm. You're awfully good at feeling your way along.

Charles: Oh, stop! I want to feel my way along you, all over you and up and down you and in and out...

Camilla: Oh!

Charles: Particularly in and out!

Camilla: Oh, that's just what I need at the moment.

Charles: Is it?

At this point the scanner enthusiast speaks over the couple to record the date.

Scanner Enthusiast: December 18th.

Camilla: I know it would revive me. I can't bear a Sunday night without you.

Charles: Oh, God.

Camilla: It's like that programme, 'Start the Week'. I can't start the week without you.

Charles: I fill up your tank!

Camilla: Yes, you do.

Charles: Then you can cope.

Camilla: Then I'm all right.

Charles: What about me? The trouble is I need you several times a week.

Camilla: Mmmm, so do I. I need you all the week. All the time.

Charles: Oh, God. I'll just live inside your trousers or something. It would be much easier!

Camilla: (*Laughing*) What are you going to turn into, a pair of knickers?

Both laugh.

Camilla: Oh, you're going to come back as a pair of knickers.

Charles: Or, God forbid, a Tampax. Just my luck! (*Laughs*)

158

Camilla: You are a complete idiot (*Laughs*). Oh, what a wonderful idea.

Charles: My luck to be chucked down the lavatory and go on and on forever swirling round on the top, never going down.

Camilla: (*Laughing*) Oh, darling!

Charles: Until the next one comes through.

Camilla: Oh, perhaps you could come back as a box.

Charles: What sort of box?

Camilla: A box of Tampax, so you could just keep going.

Charles: That's true.

Camilla: Repeating yourself...(*Laughing*) Oh, darling, I just want you now.

Charles: Do you?

Camilla: Mmmmm

Charles: So do I!

Camilla: Desperately, desperately. Oh, I thought of you so much at Garrowby.

Charles: Did you?

Camilla: Simply mean we couldn't be there together.

Charles: Desperate. If you could be here – I long to ask Nancy sometimes.

Camilla: Why don't you?

Charles: I daren't.

Camilla: Because I think she's in love with you.

Charles: Mmm.

Camilla: She'd do anything you asked.

Charles: She'd tell all sorts of people.

Camilla: No, she wouldn't because she'd be much too frightened of what you might say to her. I think you've got – I'm afraid it's a terrible thing to say – but I think, you know, those sort of people do feel very strongly about you. You've got such a hold over her.

Charles: Really?

Camilla: And you're... I think, as usual, you're underestimating yourself.

Charles: But she might be terribly jealous or something.

Camilla: Oh! (*Laughs*) Now that's a point! I wonder, she might be, I suppose.

Charles: You never know, do you?

Camilla: No, the little green-eyed monster might be lurking inside her. No, but I mean the thing is you're so good when people are so flattered to be taken into your confidence, but I don't know they'd betray you. You know, real friends.

Charles: Really?

Camilla: I don't (*Pause*)... Gone to sleep?

160

Charles: No, I'm here.

Camilla: Darling, listen, I talked to David tonight again. It might not be any good.

Charles: Oh, no!!

Camilla: I'll tell you why. He's got these children of one of those Crawley girls and their nanny staying. He's going. I'm going to ring him again tomorrow. He's going to try and put them off till Friday. But as an alternative, perhaps I might ring up Charlie.

Charles: Yes.

Camilla: And see if we could do it there. I know he is back on Thursday.

Charles: It's quite a lot further away.

Camilla: Oh, is it?

Charles: Well, I'm just trying to think. Coming from Newmarket.

Camilla:: Coming from Newmarket to me at that time of night, you could probably do it in two and three quarters, It takes me three.

Charles: What to go to, um, Bowood?

Camilla: Northmore.

Charles: To go to Bowood?

Camilla: To go to Bowood would be the same as me really, wouldn't it?

Charles: I mean to say, you would suggest going

to Bowood, uh?

Camilla: No, not at all.

Charles: Which Charlie then?

Camilla: What Charlie do you think I was talking about?

Charles: I didn't know, because I thought you meant...

Camilla: I've got lots...

Charles: Somebody else.

Camilla: I've got lots of friends called Charlie.

Charles: The other one, Patty's.

Camilla: Oh! Oh! There! Oh that is further away. They're not...

Charles: They've gone...

Camilla: I don't know. It's just, you know, just a thought I had, if it fell through, the other place.

Charles: Oh, right. What do you do? Go on the M25 then down the M4 is it?

Camilla: Yes, you go, um, and sort of Royston or M11, at that time of night.

Charles: Yes, well, that'll be just after shooting anyway.

Camilla: So it would be, um, you'd miss the worst of the traffic. Because I'll, er.... You see the problem is I've got to be in London tomorrow night.

Charles: Yes.

Camilla: Would you believe it? Because, I don't know what he's doing. He's shooting down here or something. But, darling, you wouldn't be able to ring me anyway, would you?

Charles: I might just, I mean, tomorrow night I could have done.

Camilla: Oh darling, I can't bear it. How could you have done tomorrow night?

Charles: Because I'll be (*Yawns*) working on the next speech.

Camilla: Oh no, what's the next one?

Charles: A 'Business in the Community' one, rebuilding communities.

Camilla: Oh no, when's that for?

Charles: A rather important one for Wednesday.

Camilla: Well at least I'll be behind you.

Charles: I know.

Camilla: Can I have a copy of the one you've just done?

Charles: Yes.

Camilla: Can I? Um, I would like it.

Charles: OK, I'll try and organize it.

Camilla: Darling.

Charles: But I, oh God, when am I going to speak to you?

Camilla: I can't bear it... Umm...

Charles: Wednesday night?

Camilla: Oh, certainly Wednesday night. I'll be alone, um, Wednesday, you know, the evening. Or Tuesday, while you're rushing around doing things, I'll be, you know, alone until it reappears. And early Wednesday morning, I mean, he'll be leaving at half past eight, quarter past eight. He won't be here Thursday, pray God. Um, that ambulance strike, it's a terrible thing to say this, I suppose it won't have come to an end by Thursday?

Charles: It will have done?

Camilla: Well, I mean I hope for everybody's sake it will have done, but I hope for our sakes it's still going on.

Charles: Why?

Camilla: Well, because if it stops he'll come down here on Thursday night.

Charles: Oh no.

Camilla: Yes, but I don't think it will stop, do you?

Charles: No, neither do I. Just our luck.

Camilla: It just would be our luck, I know.

Charles: Then it's bound to.

Camilla: No it won't. You mustn't think like that.

You must think positive.

Charles: I'm not very good at that.

Camilla: Well I'm going to. Because if I don't, I'd despair. (*Pause*) Hmmm – gone to sleep?

Charles: No. How maddening.

Camilla: I know. Anyway, I mean, he's doing his best to change it, David. But I just thought, you know, I might ask Charlie.

Charles: Did he say anything?

Camilla: No, I haven't talked to him.

Charles: You haven't?

Camilla: Well I talked to him briefly, but you know, I just thought I – I just don't know whether he's got any children at home, that's the worry.

Charles: Right.

Camilla: Oh, darling. I think I'll...

Charles: Pray, just pray.

Camilla: It would be so wonderful to have just one night to set us on our way, wouldn't it?

Charles: Wouldn't it? To wish you a Happy Christmas.

Camilla: (*Indistinct*) Happy. Oh, don't let's think about Christmas. I can't bear it. (*Pause*) Going to go to sleep? I think you'd better, don't you darling?

Charles: (*Sleepy*) Yes, darling.

Camilla: Will you ring me when you wake up?

Charles: Yes I will.

Camilla: Before I have these rampaging children around. It's Tom's birthday tomorrow. (*Pause*) You all right?

Charles: Mmm. I'm all right.

Camilla: Can I talk to you, I hope, before those rampaging children...

Charles: What time do they come in?

Camilla: Well, usually Tom never wakes up at all, but as it's his birthday tomorrow he might just stagger out of bed. It won't be before half past eight. (*Pause*) Night, night, my darling.

Charles: Darling...

Camilla: I do love you.

Charles: (*Sleepily*) Before...

Camilla: Before half past eight.

Charles: Try and ring?

Camilla: Yeah, if you can. Love you darling.

Charles: Night, darling.

Camilla: I love you.

Charles: I love you, too. I don't want to say good-bye.

Camilla: Well done for doing that. You're a clever old thing. An awfully good brain lurking there, isn't there? Oh, darling, I think you ought to give the brain a rest now. Night, night.

Charles: Night darling, God bless.

Camilla: I do love you and I'm so proud of you.

Charles: Oh, I'm so proud of you.

Camilla: Don't be silly. I've never achieved anything.

Charles: Your greatest achievement is to love me.

Camilla: Oh, darling, easier than falling off a chair.

Charles: You suffer all these indignities and tortures and calumnies.

Camilla: Oh, darling, don't be so silly I'd suffer anything for you. That's love. It's the strength of love. Night, night.

Charles: Night, darling. Sounds if you're dragging an enormous piece of string behind you, with hundreds of tin pots and cans attached to it. Night night, before the battery goes. (*Blows kiss*) Night.

Camilla: Love you.

Charles: Don't want to say goodbye.

Camilla: Neither do I, but you must get some sleep. Bye.

Charles: Bye, darling.

Camilla: Love you.

Charles: Bye.

Camilla: Hopefully talk to you in the morning.

Charles: Please.

Camilla: Bye, I do love you.

Charles: Night.

Camilla: Night.

Charles: Night.

Camilla: Love you forever.

Charles: Night.

Camilla: G'bye. Bye my darling.

Charles: Night.

Camilla: Night, night.

Charles: Night.

Camilla: Bye bye.

Charles: Going.

Camilla: Gone.

Charles: Going.

Camilla: Gone

Charles: Night.

Camilla: Bye. Press the button.

Charles: Going to press the tit.

Camilla: All right darling, I wish you were pressing mine.

Charles: God, I wish I was, harder and harder.

Camilla: Oh, darling.

Charles: Night.

Camilla: Night.
Charles: Love you.
Camilla: (*Yawning*) Love you. Press the tit.
Charles: Adore you. Night.
Camilla: Night.
Charles: Night.
Camilla: (*Blows a kiss*)
Charles: Night.
Camilla: G'night my darling, Love you.
Charles then finally hangs up the phone...

The Tampax bit is beyond awful. The entire workforce of this nation and other nations around the world took a long coffee break to consider how on earth, in the name of humility, Prince Charles Philip Arthur George was ever going to go out in public again. In the Fiji Islands the government announced that it wasn't going to celebrate Charles's birthday any more as he no longer represented greatness to them. And Diana, who had just moved out of Highgrove, summed up her own feelings about it when she said to Patrick Jephson, her private secretary, 'God, Patrick, a Tampax! That's sick!'

Camilla was photographed covering her head, her face all skew-whiff with emotion and the caption read 'Uncontrolled anguish and despair'. She was supposed to have been harangued in a Chippenham supermarket but her friend Jilly Cooper is adamant that 'she was never stoned by buns in Sainsbury's… that was complete fabrication by the press.'

The *Mail on Sunday* ran a story headed 'Cabinet Ministers Plea to Charles: Never See Her Again.' And in response to all this, to the world and its newspapers pontificating on whether someone who wanted to be reincarnated as sanitary protection was fit to be the future King of England, Charles let it be known that, although he thought it was the low point in the crisis, he wasn't about to make any apology or show any remorse.

He is supposed to have asked, referring to the press, 'What bloody business is it of theirs?' A valid point coming from anyone but him really, because if it is the press's business to turn out and report favourably on his fairytale wedding to his fairytale virgin bride then it is also the press's business to turn out and report the lie – 'His happiness may be private,' wrote Lesley Garner, in the *Evening Standard*, 'but publicly his marriage and his soul are everybody's business.'

'This was the sword of Damocles hanging over him,' said a friend. 'The worst is over now. Things can only get better.' Angry Cabinet ministers continued to make it clear that Prince Charles should show that he was a bit remorseful, just a teensy bit, but his camp stood firm and insisted that he would ride out the storm.

The Prince spent the weekend after the publication of Camillagate at Sandringham, where he could count on some spontaneous applause from loyal locals, who in the event overdid it a bit by shouting out 'Good old Charlie' as he made his way to Church. Charles walked next to his father who, while no doubt fuming, was complicit in this show of family solidarity.

Later the following week Charles retreated to Balmoral, to his grandmother, known as a 'good restorer of backbones'. The Romseys and the Palmer-Tomkinsons accompanied him for a council of war, which was described for the benefit of the press as a sporting weekend – the sport of wannabe kings. The Camilla facilitators, who were not at Balmoral, the other keepers of the secret and providers of the Travelodges, were plagued by journalists and asked how much they had known about the affair all along. Major

Shand said, 'I think we had better keep our traps shut.'

And then there was Camilla who was miserable and surely missing a few hours sleep, if not a whole night or two. She was apparently wracked with guilt about Andrew being forced to run the gauntlet of the press every day. The first thing she said when told by a *Sun* reporter that the transcript was to be published was: 'Oh my god, I can't believe it. I must speak to my husband.'

'For a time she thought she was the most hated woman in the country,' said a friend. 'She had hate-mail, she had crank calls and although Andrew did his best to support her, his patience was wearing thin... but what really spooked her was the idea that she was being spied on.'

There were people who thought that those responsible for the bugging were rogue cells of army or navy intelligence. There was a government enquiry into the affair but, in late March 1993, John Major published two official reports that cleared M15 and the intelligence agencies. In the end, the general feeling was that the conversation had been recorded and leaked by a mole in the security services. Prince Charles swapped his cellular phone for one with an inbuilt scrambling device, which was prudent if not terribly remorseful.

In the week following the publication of Camillagate, he had encountered an indignant pensioner in a London health centre who had shouted, 'Have you no shame?' Charles, cupping his hand around his not insubstantial ear, had asked the indignant pensioner to repeat what he'd said. 'Have you no shame?' said the indignant pensioner. Charles got into his car.

Three weeks later Camillagate was still up and running and becoming an industry in its own right. On 1st February snippets of the tape were broadcast in America, interspersed with comments from Richard Kay, the *Daily Mail* royal correspondent and friend of Diana's, and Harry Arnold of the *Daily Mirror*. The *Los Angeles Times* described Camillagate as the 'most widely read royal document since the Magna Carta'.

What made it so gripping, and also poignant, once the initial sense of repulsion had evaporated was not just the Prince's Tampax aspiration. It was the depth of feeling he and Camilla displayed for each other; the sheer desperate frisson of frustration they gave off about not being able to see each other. It is a very sexy late night phone call between two in-love-and-lust lovers given magnificent dramatic emphasis by Camilla's long, drawn-out, lugubrious drawl.

There is that sexual groan at the idea of Charles feeling his way along, a blissfully '*Carry On*-esque' *double entendre*: 'Mmm. You're awfully good feeling your way along.'

'Oh stop!,' says Charles. 'I want to feel my way along you, all over you and up and down you and in and out.'

'Oh!' says Camilla.

'Particularly in and out!' says Charles.

Sid James eat your heart out. But there is more. There is the loyalty and admiration demonstrated by Camilla and the desperate, desperate gratitude from Charles. As one writer put it: 'A greater love hath no woman than to lay down an afternoon for a tract on the social responsibility of business,' and for all Diana's thoughtfulness and consideration for others – the sick and the dying and the troubled – it is hard to imagine her making this sort of sacrifice for her husband, even if he had been a loving and faithful one. It is hard to imagine her volunteering to read one of Prince Charles's speeches. It is hard to imagine anyone who isn't actually in the pay of Prince Charles laying down an afternoon to read one of Prince Charles's speeches. It must be bad enough for the innocent citizens of the world who have to go along and listen to him giving one of his speeches.

But Camilla's mother love is, it would seem, unconditional – not blind – she must see his faults – it's just that they do not interfere with her unconditional love for him. 'I do love you and I'm so proud of you,' she says.

'Oh, I'm so proud of you.'
'Don't be silly. I've never achieved anything.'
'Your greatest achievement is to love me.'
'Oh, darling, easier than falling off a chair.'
'You suffer all these indignities and tortures and calumnies.'
'Oh, darling, don't be so silly I'd suffer anything for you. That's love. It's the strength of love. Night, night.'

And then there are the misunderstandings, the moments when they stumble over each other. He thought that she meant one particular Charlie when in fact she meant another Charlie. There were the considerations they had to make, the convoluted safety precautions: which house; which

Camilla facilitator; which exit off the M4 depending on the traffic; the possibility that there might be children staying – children who would see Prince Charles and his girlfriend together and tell on them at school; the furtive wish that the ambulance strike would continue so that Andrew would be too busy with his soldiers to come home to his errant wife. This conversation gives us one, brief glimpse of the lengths to which two people in love were forced to go, throughout most of their affair, just to be together. They weren't supposed to be together, it was against the rules, so there was the guilt but also the excitement, which is why, after all these years, they still breathed heavily when they spoke to each other and called each other darling 23 times in one phone call.

Chapter Twelve

Everyone assumed that Camillagate would damn Charles to eternal disgrace, but it didn't. He survived it. The press would go back to it every so often: when the Parker Bowleses were seen together; when Camilla ducked and dived behind Tom and Andrew during a day at the races; when Andrew and Camilla went to a race meeting at Cheltenham; when Camilla didn't go with Andrew to Birkhall; when the security arrangements at Middlewick House were suddenly made state of the art.

A story surfaced which portrayed Prince Charles as a shame-faced and tearful, admonished boy. Apparently Major Shand summoned Charles to tell him to leave his daughter alone and when the Prince said he would think about it, and the

Major said, 'You will not think about it, you will do it,' the Prince burst into tears.

Every so often, then, the spectre of the tampon would hover. But Charles kept his official engagements and managed to duck for cover whenever an indignant pensioner hove into view. He kept seeing Camilla and phoning her. They were indefatigable, nothing would deter them, they were addicted to each other, they couldn't help themselves. The opinion polls said they thought it would be for the best if we ignored hopeless Charles and went straight to handsome, Spencer-blooded William.

It is impossible to imagine what it must have been like to be Camilla Parker Bowles during this time. She tried to be normal, she went on holiday to India with some girlfriends, including Dame Shirley Porter, which perhaps wasn't so normal. She led her life but she couldn't ignore the fact that her children were being teased at school; her husband was having a terrible year; her lover, needy at the best of times, must have been permanently on the phone or around her neck; and then, when, as she inevitably must have done, she heard or read that everyone from the Archbishop of Canterbury to the Prime Minister and his Cabinet ministers were talking about what she and Charles had done, she must occasionally have put down her trug basket and buried her face in the neck of a Labrador, or the mane of a handy hunter, and bawled.

And she didn't even have her Prince to turn to, because she loved him too much and he had enough problems of his own. She had to be motherly, and not cry. His friends said Prince Charles was renowned for his very steady and absorbent shoulder but Camilla wouldn't cry on it. She had to be the carer. It couldn't be the other way round.

There were those who said she was *too* motherly and manipulative and that in fact, far from sobbing and regretting, she was getting uppity about the palace attempts to bring Charles and Diana's working relationship on to a steady footing. Although, after Camillagate, it seemed inevitable that the Parker Bowleses would divorce, they issued a statement saying they wouldn't: 'We will never divorce. It is not something that has been considered,' they said. But still everyone thought they probably would, in the end, and what then? Would the Waleses divorce, too? Would Charles and Camilla marry? Would Camilla be queen? Camilla has always laughed at the idea of being queen. She thinks it's hilarious, a joke. A friend said, 'She has no desire for position or power. She's as unlike Mrs Simpson as you could possibly be, and certainly has no wish to be queen.' No, being queen wasn't the idea at all, although over the years Camilla has certainly gained position and power. Her love affair has made her powerful, and powerful people talk about her.

While the Archbishop of Canterbury, Dr George Carey, said divorce should be looked on 'more positively' and could sometimes lead to better relationships, others were less accommodating about the Prince of Wales's marital and extramarital affairs. The Archbishop of York, Dr John Habgood, said 'all tolerance has its limits.' And in December 1993 the Archdeacon of York, the Venerable George Austin, said on the radio:

Does he [Charles] have the right to be trusted with the role of king, if his attitude to matrimony is so cavalier? Prince Charles made solemn vows before God in church about his marriage, and it seems he began to break them almost immediately... How can he then go into church, into Westminster Abbey, and take the coronation vows?... Are we to believe him that he will keep those? It brings into question the whole attitude of Charles to vows, trust, and so on. The Church forgives of course; if I as Archdeacon of York fiddled the books or cheated on my wife or broke my ordination vows, God would forgive me if I repented. But I might be totally unsuitable at the end of it to be Archdeacon of York.

In his biography of Charles, Jonathan Dimbleby was to report that the Venerable George Austin was 'a minor cleric of Pickwickian demeanour and modest accomplishment'. Still, plenty followed his lead: the Bishop of Sodor and Man, the Bishop of Kensington, the Suffragen Bishop to the Diocese of Exeter... And when the Venerable George Austin then repeated his feelings in an article in the *Times*, Charles's camp – as represented by the Prince's friend Nicholas Soames – blundered into the frame:

What he [George Austin] has said is a disgrace. The suggestion that being heir to the throne is a lottery is completely inappropriate. To be heir to the throne is not an ambition, but is a duty and an obligation, which will befall the Prince of Wales at a sad moment later in his life... He will inherit the throne; that is the end of the matter. It's not like being a football manager when you shake the pack and see who will fall out... What was said today was utterly outrageous. I am very surprised by what this man has said – it is disgraceful, wounding, ignorant and hurtful... I do not think the vaporings of a completely unrepresentative archdeacon will make any difference. But it was still quite, quite disgraceful.

Archdeacon Austin did make a difference though; he prompted a survey in the Synod. Forty-seven per cent of Synod members thought the Prince of Wales should not become supreme governor of the Church of England when he became king. Twenty-seven per cent thought he should not become king at all. Even Camilla's father, devoted and loyal though he was and still is to his daughter, had a little dig, when he said in an interview in answer to a question about sexual permissiveness, 'It's a pity that the ties of marriage have been so destroyed by it. Has the country gone to the dogs?'

Shand echoed precisely what most men and women of his age, the backbone of middle England, were thinking: that the country, as personified by the heir to the throne, had well and truly gone to the dogs.

So Soames's 'Don't-be-mean-about-my-friend-Prince-Charles' rant had no effect whatsoever, other than to highlight Charles's failure to show any remorse. The newspaper leader writers, meanwhile, were quick to point out the irony that Charles was set to be defender of the very faith that King Henry VIII had founded in order to get rid of his first wife.

Ten years later – after Diana, after it was well known that Camilla was sharing Charles's life at St James's and Highgrove – Austin changed his mind and wrote an article in the *Daily Mail* headed 'Why Charles and Camilla should marry'.

The view in the Cabinet, meanwhile, was that Charles's self-imposed silence had done him unnecessary damage. Throughout this Camillagate year, the spinners at Prince Charles's newly established St James's press office, headed by Commander Richard Aylard, had tried to turn things around, but with little or no help from the Prince. The *Daily Telegraph* did what they could under the headline 'The Prince of Wales Chooses the Celibate Life', and the *Daily Express* was persuaded to run a story headed 'Charles Gave Up

Camilla 2 Years Ago'. The story claimed that the Prince had decided to put duty before love, that it was Diana who had refused a reconciliation and that 45-year-old Camilla, 'now beginning to lose her looks', could not cope with being dumped by the man 'she cherished'.

'The Prince made a gentleman's agreement with Brigadier Parker Bowles never to see his wife again,' said the *Express*.

In fact, Andrew Parker Bowles was now seeing a lot of his old, bosom friend Princess Anne. She had just divorced Captain Mark Phillips and 'Andrew felt free to help Anne through this bad patch,' said a friend.

There were rumours that they became lovers again. Indeed, as recently as spring 2003, there were whisperings that Anne and Andrew were seeing each other romantically again – they were at Cheltenham Races together unveiling a tribute to the Queen Mother: '...the lines between friendship and rekindled passion were blurred, Gatcombe Park being rather closer to the fabled racecourse than Andrew's home near Malmesbury,' wrote the *Daily Mail*.

Post Camillagate, Andrew also saw a lot of an old flame called Countess Peel. She was, before her various marriages, Charlotte Soames, sister of Nicholas Soames, defender of Charles after Camillagate – another example of a Camilla social circle – and Andrew had been an aide-de-camp to her father, Lord Soames, in Rhodesia in the late 1970s until independence in 1980. Prince Charles went to Rhodesia, incidentally, in 1980, the last of the pre-Diana days, for the independence celebrations and scheduled into his programme was a ride on a buffalo called Ziggy. Andrew Parker Bowles was worried for the Prince's safety so he gave Ziggy a trial run and was thrown and gored. Before being carried off to hospital he gave instructions that the Prince's buffalo ride should be scrubbed from the itinerary. Another reason for Charles to be eternally grateful to his girlfriend's husband.

Andrew was said to be in love with Charlotte Soames and they remained friends. So there was no shortage of old flames for the cuckolded and battered old thing to call in on after Camillagate, during his own particular *annus horribilis*. He wasn't having a great time on the career front either. He was given a new job as director of the Royal Army Veterinary Corps and because in its 200-year-old history it had never been led by anyone other than a qualified vet there were angry stirrings in the ranks. The Corps' colonel resigned and wrote a petulant letter to the Ministry of Defence.

Parker Bowles kept the job, with the proviso that he would be merely a director who managed the troops: he would not interfere with any veterinary procedures. The rumblings that this was an appointment of convenience, that there were others who weren't married to the Prince of Wales's mistress who would have been more suited, were ignored, but it must have been an uncomfortable time for the stoic Brigadier, especially since he had forged such a brilliant career to date.

The Parker Bowlses's circle of dear, close friends were being stoic too – still insisting that a divorce would be unheard of. Any suggestion of it was greeted with puffed-up splutters and brays of disbelief. Lord Beaverbrook, a cousin of Andrew Parker Bowles, thundered, 'This is totally preposterous. Anyone who knows Andrew will understand that he will stand by his wife in these difficult times.' Simon Parker Bowles, Andrew's brother, said, 'They will never divorce and while the relationship is rather eccentric, it appears to work. They get on well.' A friend said that theirs was a 'rock solid partnership. Dynamite couldn't blow them apart.'

'Camilla wasn't a good army wife,' said a friend of Andrew's, 'precisely because she couldn't stand all the regalia and buttering up.' She was never around Andrew the soldier much, so she wasn't suddenly missed in military circles when she went to ground after Camillagate. She was seen in public occasionally, looking wan and tired. A friend said, 'I am genuinely worried about her. The spark has gone out of her life and she looks haunted and hunted.'

In March 1993, with Diana gone from Highgrove, Charles and Camilla began redecorating – Robert Kime was brought in to mess it up a bit – de-swag it. Diana had filled the house with the interior design equivalent of the pie-frill blouse and velvet knickerbocker and all that had to go – the sofas needed some metaphorical dog hair and Kime was the man whom Camilla, the surrogate lady of the house, hired for the job.

Charles and Camilla have always had Highgrove. Even during the years of Diana's occupancy, Camilla was still a presence in the house; she was there when the Princess and William and Harry weren't. She pottered about there in the same way she pottered about her own garden with dogs trailing around after her. Her horses were stabled at Highgrove; she rode around the Highgrove estate; and she swam in the Highgrove swimming-pool. She and Charles had painting lessons at Highgrove. A friend of the Prince's and Camilla's said once, 'She doesn't share many of his artistic tastes. She'll say at a Highgrove dinner, "This isn't going to be one of those bloody musical evenings, is it?" But she embodies a lot of the things Charles was familiar with in his childhood... the way she sits on a horse, her skill with a fishing rod, her passion for gardening.'

And now Diana, who had never been keen on sitting on horses, fishing or gardening, had gone, so while there was always the danger of the staff, Ken Stronach for instance, turning traitor, at least the furious, rampaging Princess was out of the way. Highgrove was peaceful and the gardens which made Camilla's favourite little Prince happy were lovely.

At the end of 1993, Spode china produced a porcelain figurine called Camilla. She was eight and three quarter inches high and cost £165. She looked a bit like the real Camilla – same hair, and she came with a heart-rending little story: 'She

had a secret admirer, but strict social etiquette for-
bids her talking to him, or even acknowledging
him.' So it wasn't all gloom and doom, there were
some things still to laugh at and still honey from
the Highgrove bees for tea.

Chapter Thirteen

In January 1994, when Charles was giving prizes in Sydney to two Australian 'schoolchildren of the year', a man protesting about the Cambodian boat people ran at him firing blanks from a pistol. Charles remained calm and self-possessed as David Kang was brought down by security men. He wrote later, 'I thought it must be one of the prize winners who was particularly keen to receive his trophy!'

If the palace spinners had set the whole thing up it couldn't have worked better. When Charles set off on his Australian tour, one year on from Camillagate, he was at an all-time low in the polls; the day after the Kang incident, he was a hero.

Meanwhile, back in England, a band of friends had taken it upon themselves to put out a story saying that Charles had dumped Camilla. It was known as the 'Tippex the Tampax' campaign, or the 'Ditch the Bitch' campaign – but probably not something to which either Charles or Camilla or even the Queen were party. The result of it was that any good that had been done by the Prince's apparent bravery over Kang was swiftly undone.

Nigel Dempster was the man chosen to write the story. It was headlined 'Prince Charles Severs all Links', and it said that the Prince had chosen to 'fulfil his destiny as future king by renouncing Mrs Parker Bowles'. Dempster reported that Charles was no longer taking Camilla's calls.

Dempster was wrong. Charles was taking Camilla's calls. He was taking them and making them. They were long calls from the other side of the world to the unbugged house of a friend in the English shires where Camilla would go, in much the same way as, in the days before mobile phones, ordinary people might nip to a nearby call-box if for some reason the phone at home wasn't working.

One quite plausible explanation for the 'Ditch the Bitch' story, which, when it appeared, made Charles very angry, is that the friends knew that Charles and Camilla wanted to be able to be seen

at the same events – polo, hunting, the races, parties, weddings. The theory was that, if everyone
thought they weren't girlfriend and boyfriend any
more, it wouldn't matter if they both went out
with, for instance, the Beaufort, on the same day
as each other rather than on alternate days.

But the plan didn't work. It was bad enough
that Charles had a mistress at all, but now this
latest, misguided effort by some well-meaning
friends made him look like the kind of man who
would dump someone who had been doggedly and
relentlessly loyal to him. 'It is totally out of character,' said a friend who was hauled in to put
things back as they had been. 'He is a very loyal
man. As the rest of his world has fallen apart, he
needs Camilla more than ever.'

'He won't ever deny her,' said another friend
lyrically.

A woman, waiting to see the Prince outside St
David's Cathedral in Hobart, Tasmania, said
'Diana was the best ambassador the royal family
could ever have. She had such silky skin.' And on
the same day, back in England, Camilla, the not
so silky one, the one the female columnists called
'leathery', took cups of coffee to some workmen
chopping logs in her field. She smiled at the nosey

pressmen, made sure they saw the coffee mugs which had 'Love' written on them, made sure they clocked her daughter and some friends having a lovely time on quad bikes and made sure they saw her walking 'side by side' with Andrew around the garden. She wasn't looking like a woman who had been dumped. She was looking like a woman who, while her high-maintenance lover was away, was having a nice day at home in the country with her family who she also loved – just in a different way.

***

1994 was the 25th anniversary of Charles's investiture – time, then, for an authorized biography. Jonathan Dimbleby had been chosen and Charles seemed keen. There was lots he wanted to talk about: The Prince's Trust, the Duchy, the farm at Highgrove. Apart from his catastrophically awful marriage, his life hadn't been so bad – he was a hard worker, he believed in his destiny and his duty to his country. He had a good story to tell – his sad and tortured childhood, his action man naval career, the polo, the travels, the spiritualism and gardening and definite views on architecture.

Camilla, who was having a better year so far

after the terrible '92 and '93, was not at all keen. She had not been keen since the thing was first mooted, and she was no keener now as there began to be talk of a television interview. To Camilla's mind, it seemed downright silly to go stirring the pot now. There were a few little stories in the press at this time but they were quite harmless, and, in the case of poor Pooh, the Prince's missing Jack Russell, who was a brother of Camilla's own Jack Russell, Freddy, rather endearing. The story was revived a while later when it was learnt that Camilla's Freddy then fathered a puppy who became Pooh's replacement. The puppy was called Tosca but she was horrid to another dog called Tigger, so in the end she was found a new home. *Daily Mail* readers just love this sort of stuff.

The stories in the papers at this time were so minor that Camilla herself felt relaxed enough to hand the press another minor story on a plate when she went to San Lorenzo, a restaurant in Knightsbridge, which was where Diana went to meet James Gilbey of Squidgeygate fame. It was where soap stars and footballers went with their wives. So you can only imagine that Camilla went for a joke, for a hoot. She was back on form, and now Charles was going to make things appalling again with an authorized biography.

Even a good sort of a person, a one-of-us kind of chap like Dimbleby would want to ask about the mistress. And what was Charles going to say? Perhaps he would deny her after all. Nigel Dempster wrote that Camilla had pleaded 'tearfully' with Charles not to co-operate with a biography but he wouldn't listen. She asked him to at the very least tell his advisors, among them his private secretary, Commander Richard Aylard, about how worried she was. But it made no difference. They, especially Aylard, agreed with the Prince and so Dimbleby went ahead and Charles handed over bundles of his hand-wringing letters as evidence of his well-meaning, hard-done-by life.

In March 1994, Prince Charles gave a 25th anniversary of investiture interview to *Newsnight*. A chunk of what he said was copied verbatim into an article in the *Los Angeles Times* – the writer's aim was to show what a muddled mind the heir to the British throne seemed to have. It is interesting because it demonstrates precisely why Camilla was so worried, not just for her own privacy but for her Prince's reputation. It also shows how heroic Camilla is that she has listened to him for all these years and yet still stands firmly by. Prince Charles is not an articulate man.

This is him talking about his goals in life:

> I think, more than anything else, what I'm trying to do is to encourage a more holistic approach to many of the issues which I think are important. I happen to feel that since the 1960s, a great deal of destructiveness has taken place in terms of throwing the baby out with the bathwater, in many of the things that matter, certainly to me and I think to an awful lot of other people. All I want to do is bring the baby back, which got chucked out in the process. Which is one of the reasons why, for instance, I started my institute of architecture. Why I took an interest in architectural matters. Because again, I think it needs again a more holistic approach. Same thing with agriculture. I believe that a great deal needs to be done there to create amore holistic approach. Same with medicine. So I believe that all these things are part of my particular approach to trying to bring the baby back with the bathwater having chucked the bathwater out.

Camilla did what she often does when she is

worried about something: she went on holiday with friends. This time it was to Malaga, with the Marquess and Marchioness of Douro. But her trip was cut short. She returned to England to be near her 72-year-old mother.

Rosalind Shand, like Sonia Cubitt before her, had osteoporosis, and in July 1994 she died in a private hospital in Sussex. She had been married to Major Shand for 48 years. Camilla once described her as a 'pillar of strength' and a 'model of discretion'.

Eight years later, as a patron of the National Osteoporosis Society, Camilla gave a speech. She said,

I became involved with osteoporosis after my mother and grandmother both tragically died as a result of this crippling disease. My mother was only 72. Then, only eight years ago, osteoporosis was seldom discussed and rarely diagnosed and usually attributed to old women with 'dowager's hump'. My family knew nothing. We watched in horror as she quite literally shrunk in front of our eyes. She lost about eight inches in height and became so bent she was unable to digest her food properly, leaving her with no appetite at all. I believe that the quality of her life became so dismal and her suffering so unbearable that she just gave up the fight and lost the will to live.

Rosalind Shand once said of her daughter: 'I think Camilla has done remarkably well, considering the terrible things written about her.' Camilla was the last to arrive at the funeral service at East Chiltington and the first to leave. The people Mrs Shand had been referring to, the reporters who had written such terrible things, lined the lanes leading to the church.

On 29th June 1994, Prince Charles's interview with Jonathan Dimbleby was broadcast as part of an ITV documentary, 'Charles: The Private Man, The Public Role', and the next day we were all talking about Camilla again. We were also talking about how fantastic the Princess of Wales looked when she went to a *Vanity Fair* party at the Serpentine Gallery wearing a particularly sensational dress on the same evening that her husband was confessing adultery to a television audience of fourteen million people. And the contrast to the peachy Princess was downtrodden, cowed and anguished Camilla, and her by now very angry husband.

Jonathan Dimbleby wrote in a revised version of his biography published in 1998 that what the people saw was 'evidently a revelation: that the Prince was thoughtful, sensitive and intelligent, that he had quick wit and a warm way with all manner of people, that he had a daunting range of commitments, that he was diligent, and that he was driven by a powerful sense of duty and destiny.'

According to a *Chicago Tribune* writer, on the other hand, all Prince Charles appeared to have to do was 'cut some ribbons, read some speeches, launch a few ships, make casual nice-nice with a lot of people, have clean fingernails, dress well, and show up on time.' Before the Dimbleby documentary this was the general consensus. Dimbleby was right, though – the polls and letters and calls to newsdesks did show that the Prince had gone down well in the programme and it was odd and unexpected because of that confession that he had betrayed the beautiful girl in the amazing dress.

Dimbleby said, 'You were, because of your relationship with Camilla Parker Bowles, from the beginning persistently unfaithful to your wife and thus caused the breakdown.'

Charles said, 'I mean, there is no truth in so

much of this speculation, and Mrs Parker Bowles is a great friend of mine.'

Dimbleby asked whether he tried to be 'faithful and honourable' to his wife, and he said: 'Yes, absolutely.'

'And you were?'

'Yes... until it became irretrievably broken down, us both having tried.'

Dimbleby put it to the Prince that his relationship with Mrs Parker Bowles had been the cause of the breakdown of his marriage from the very start. 'What is your response to that persistent criticism?' he asked.

'That's the persistent criticism, is it?' said Charles, 'Well I, the trouble is, you see, that these things again, as I was saying earlier, are so personal that it's difficult to know quite how to... you know, to talk about these things in front of everybody and obviously I don't think many people would want to. But I mean, all I can say is there's been so much speculation and feeding on every other kind of speculation so it all becomes bigger and bigger; but all I can say is, um... that, I mean, there is no truth in, in so much of this speculation, and Mrs Parker Bowles is a great friend of mine and I have a large number of friends. I am terribly lucky to have so many friends who I think are wonderful and make the whole difference to my life, which would become intolerable otherwise. And she has been a friend for a very long time and, along with other friends, and will continue to be a friend for a very long time and I think also most people, probably, would... would realize that when their marriages break down, awful and miserable as that is, that, so often, you know, it is your friends who are the most important and helpful and understanding and encouraging, otherwise you would go stark, raving mad and that's what friends are for.'

On the subject of his broken marriage the Prince continued, 'It's the last possible thing that I ever wanted to happen. It's not something that I went into... marriage, you know, with the intention of this happening, or in a way in a cynical frame of mind. I mean, I'm, on the whole, not a cynical person and, you know, it sounds self-righteous to say so, but I have on the whole tried to get it right.'

It is hard to believe that he had had months to rehearse this. It is hard to believe that he went down so well in the polls the next day. The Scout Association wasn't so happy. It said: 'We extol the virtues of honesty, integrity and the sanctity of marriage. But Prince Charles does not represent those virtues.'

The newspaper editors weren't expecting any sympathy for Prince Charles, as was demonstrated by the following day's headlines. 'Another Error of Judgment', said the *Mail*. ('Another' referred to an incident which had occurred on the same day as the ITV broadcast when the Prince overshot a runway and steered a Queen's Flight jet into a Hebridean bog.) The *Sun* reported that readers had jammed its switchboard because 'they did not want an adulterer on the throne'. *Today* newspaper said Charles was 'Prince of Whines'. The *Mirror* said he was 'not fit to reign'.

But they got it completely wrong: the public loved Prince Charles, confession and all, and the following day they were forced to change the story. 'Charles rules OK', said the *Sun*. So it didn't seem to be a disaster at all for Charles as he fished and frolicked in front of telephoto lenses with William and Harry in Scotland.

For Camilla, though, it was hell all over again. One friend said, post-Dimbleby, 'She has behaved admirably in a horrific situation which has been caused solely by the Prince in his urge to clear his conscience. Frankly, he has behaved like a pig and landed Camilla right in it. She has done absolutely nothing to deserve this after all the support she has given him over the years through difficult times.' Andrew Parker Bowles was said to be 'galled and upset'.

The weekend after the broadcast, Camilla and Laura were at Middlewick House surrounded by photographers. One family friend said, 'In all the years I have known Camilla – and her husband Andrew – she has never once mentioned her feelings for the Prince or if she has any ambitions in that direction. Obviously she is resilient. You would have to be in that situation. Maybe she has some great plan but she has never mentioned it to me, and not even to her husband.'

The husband is often the last to know but surely, despite his denials to the press down the years, Andrew Parker Bowles had been in on it, knew what the grand plan was. Apparently not. He knew his wife was sleeping with the Prince of Wales, he knew he and Camilla had an open marriage, but, according to this anonymous friend, he really did think that they could all bowl happily along for years to come without changing anything. He really, genuinely didn't think he was going to get divorced.

In the wake of the Dimbleby interview, the papers filled up with those stories from Camilla's grandmother's butler and Highgrove employees who had witnessed moonlit trysts and muddy pyjamas. But no one took any notice.

We were suffering a surfeit of royal gossip. We felt, as Major Shand did, that the country had gone to the dogs. There was still plenty of speculation about the right to succession and morganatic marriages; Archbishops said their pieces; Archdeacon Austin praised Charles for his courage in confessing; and Camilla hunkered down at Middlewick for the duration. 'Charles has locked her in, and thrown away the key,' said a friend.

She did sometimes get to the supermarket. One day in Sainsbury's, as she stood at the checkout, a man asked 'Who's paying for that lot then, the taxpayers?' His friend said, 'Where's Charlie then, waiting at home for you? I hope you're paying for all that yourself.'

But mostly she stayed in or escaped across the fields to a waiting car, which would take her to Highgrove. She wore, like Toad, her cleaning lady's headscarf, a prank which she probably thought was quite funny, light relief, as she surfaced and threw off her disguise and plomped herself down on a sofa in Charles's drawing-room.

And, meanwhile, Andrew was getting angrier and angrier, not about the affair but about the television confession. Charles had broken the rules. In November 1994 Simon Parker Bowles, Andrew's brother, and his wife Carolyn gave an interview to an Australian magazine. They said that Camilla had been 'dropped in a heap', by Charles – poor Camilla in a heap at Middlewick. Simon Parker Bowles said that Charles was wrong to have whined about his upbringing and blamed his parents and he said it 'must be heartbreaking for the Queen, who has really done her job so well'. Simon Parker Bowles was speaking his mind. His outburst was not at all in the same vein as the footling Nicholas Soames's defence of Charles after Camillagate. This was a member of the upper classes talking about something, which in his robust, no-nonsense view was 'just not done'. Perhaps he did have Andrew Parker Bowles's blessing to say it but it is more likely that he just thought he would help out and put the record straight on a few important points.

Prince Charles then appeared in a television documentary about his global travels, and made a joke about his sex life. He was handed a glass of camel's milk by an Arab host who told him the milk was an aphrodisiac. Charles replied 'Fat lot of use that is going to be to me, I can tell you.'

Camilla rose above it and went on holiday again – to Kenya, with her friend Fiona, Lady Shelburne, plus Kirsty Smallwood, and a Norwegian businessman called Halvor Astrup and his wife. Astrup paid for the flights. They stayed at Lewa Downs which, a tabloid paper helpfully reminded us, was where the actress Stefanie Powers had married the actor Patrick de la Chesnais. And a month after Camilla returned from Kenya, in December 1994, she and Andrew filed for divorce. On 10th January 1995, they announced the end of their 21-year marriage. Andrew was 56, Camilla was 47:

> The decision to seek an end to our marriage was taken jointly and is a private matter, but as we have no expectation that our privacy will be respected, we issue this statement in the hope that it will ensure that our family and friends are saved from harassment. Most especially we ask that our children, who remain our principal concern and responsibility, are left alone to pursue

their studies at what is clearly a difficult time for them. Throughout our marriage we have always tended to follow rather different interests, but in recent years we have led completely separate lives. We have grown apart to such an extent that, with the exception of our children and a lasting friendship, there is little of common interest between us, and therefore we have decided to seek a divorce.

In fact, they had already been separated for three years and had spent no more than 90 nights under the same roof during that time.

The press gathered around Middlewick house, as they always did on these occasions, but the place was deserted; all they found was a note for the milkman that read, 'No milk until Saturday.' Andrew and Camilla had gone their separate ways. She to Highgrove, he to his future second wife, Rosemary Pitman, who lived in a pretty house in Malmesbury. Andrew and Camilla were right about the children having a difficult time. Tom Parker Bowles was having a particularly rough ride and Camilla, who felt desperate for him, visited him often after he went up to Oxford in November 1994. Another student at Worcester

College said, 'There were lots of taunts. You can imagine the kind of thing that drunken students are saying to his face and behind his back about his mother... Usually after the first week you never see parents around here, but Tom's mother must be really worried to visit him so often. The rest of the time he seems to have almost turned into a recluse. Tom's such a nice chap.' The same student also said that Tom's views about his godfather, the Prince, were unprintable. A friend of Camilla's said as recently as May 2003 that the Prince was generally disliked by all the younger members of the Parker Bowles family, including cousins, nephews and nieces. They call him something other than Prince Charles, also with the initials P. C.

Tom called himself 'Tom Bowles' at Oxford which probably helped when he was first introduced to people but it wouldn't have taken long for them to realise whose child he was, whose godchild he was. When confronted by the press, he simply said 'I've really nothing to say. I'm perfectly happy. I'm just getting on with life here.' He seemed to take the head-in-the-sand attitude his father had taken for so many years and which, for Andrew Parker Bowles, suddenly became untenable after the Dimbleby confession.

This time, after her divorce, Camilla did not go to ground. She no longer hid from the cameras – she smiled at them.

Chapter Fourteen

In November 1995 the Princess of Wales gave her interview to Martin Bashir. She said, 'There were three of us in this marriage so it was a bit crowded.' And no sooner did she say it than Camilla was put back under house arrest again by the media. Nicholas Soames blundered back on to the telly and put Diana's behaviour down to 'a period of unhappiness, that led to instability and mental illness'. He said she was 'in the advanced stages of paranoia'.

The public did not like it. The public were furious with both Charles and Camilla. Poor Camilla, back in a heap at Middlewick. Four weeks later, the Queen, after consultation with the Prime Minister and the Archbishop of Canterbury, wrote personally to both the Prince and Princess of

Wales requesting that they divorce quite soon and on Wednesday 28th February 1996, a date Diana described as 'the saddest day of my life', the Princess announced her decision to agree to an uncontested divorce.

It was also at the beginning of 1996 that the real Camilla Campaign began. She was now installed for most of the time at either Highgrove or St James's. She had rooms in both places, she had possessions in both places and she had people working on her behalf. She was described as being in charge of domestic matters – dinner-parties and flower-arranging and the staff called her 'M'lady' to her face and 'Mrs P.' behind her back.

Mark Bolland was the man brought in by Charles and his private secretary Stephen Lamport. (Richard Aylard had been sacked when the post-Dimbleby gloss started to fade and in hindsight the whole thing seemed to have been a terrible idea after all.) Bolland's mission was to promote the Prince's mistress with the public, to make the people like her and accept her, and not just her, but *her and him,* them as a couple. He had been director of the Press Complaints Commission before he went to work for Charles and Camilla full-time. He had a powerful influence and even though, eight years later, he resigned to start his own company and was no longer officially employed by Charles or Camilla, he remains someone she still speaks to pretty much every day, sometimes several times a day.

The fact that he does is interesting because Bolland went on to become not just a freelance PR but a press pundit. In 2003, at the time of the publication of Paul Burrell's biography and also as some pretty seedy stories were emerging from other former servants, Bolland felt the Prince's lot were making a merry hash of things. So he spoke out in the *Daily Mail*, in the *Sunday Times*, the *Guardian* and finally via his own weekly column in the *News of the World*. Presumably, all that he wrote had Camilla's approval – or at the very least she had agreed to turn a blind eye. It is touching to know that he keeps a framed, signed photograph of Camilla at the home he shares with Guy Black, the former Director of the Press Complaints Commission, and also to bear in mind that Camilla is, these days, with her blonde frosting, something of a gay icon.

During his days at St James's palace Mark Bolland showed that he knew how to work the press. He would feed little snippets to editors and royal correspondents and, if they behaved well and told the story favourably, he would feed them more. When Camilla met her daughter off a train at Chippenham station, it turned into what looked for all the world like an official photocall after a well-spoken woman phoned a few newspaper picture desks. Camilla turned up looking uncharacteristically tidy in a cream skirt and navy blazer. The really well-behaved newspaper editors would be let right into the inner Charles and Camilla sanctum, invited to parties, encouraged to become friends with Camilla.

Rebekah Wade, when she became editor of the *News of the World* (she is now the Editor of the *Sun*), was one. Her boyfriend Ross Kemp is a patron of the National Osteoporosis Society. So is Camilla. Kemp was also a childhood neighbour of Guy Black, the man who succeeded Bolland as director of the Press Complaints Commission. Guy Black is Mark Bolland's boyfriend – and so there starts forming a completely new and rather more multi-faceted kind of Camilla social circle. Princes William and Harry call Mark Bolland 'Blackadder'.

It was in Rebekah Wade's paper that a very

grainy photograph of Prince Charles and Camilla together was published. It was not a particularly interesting photo – it wasn't the one the world's press were waiting for because you couldn't make Charles and Camilla out; they were just pixilated lumps and anyway by this time it was pretty much accepted that they were still an item – so where was the news?

According to the other newspapers, and to the 'kiss and yell' merchant Max Clifford, the news was in the tip-off. Charles and Camilla were photographed in August 1996 walking around the gardens of Nick Paravicini's house in Wales. Max Clifford claimed he knew the couple had posed for the photograph. There were rumours that it was published as the result of a deal in which Clifford promised not to publish another photo of Camilla in a dressing-gown. A spokesman for the *News of the World* said, 'The information that led us to secure these pictures is surrounded by intrigue. A well-spoken woman [her again] contacted the paper to say that the Prince and Mrs Parker Bowles would be there.'

The story ran for a few days, there was shock and concern expressed that the Prince might have colluded in some way, and then a seven foot high fence was put along a 400-yard stretch of new bypass to protect the Paravacini property from further intrusion. But the local people of Felinfach complained, especially since it had cost the taxpayer rather than Charles or the Paravicinis. So the fence was taken down in 1998 and they planted trees instead – another obscure consequence of funny old Camilla's affair with Prince Charles. Or perhaps the plaque next to the trees should bear a dedication to Mark Bolland.

In 1996, shortly after Bolland's arrival, the phrase 'non-negotiable' began cropping up in stories about Camilla. This was apparently how Charles regarded her – she was a 'non-negotiable' part of his life. 'The Prince is understood to have made it known to senior advisers that, while he is anxious to improve his public standing, the question of Mrs Parker Bowles is non-negotiable,' said a senior advisor/Bolland. The people were finally on message.

Except that in March 1996, at Spitalfields, a man who wished the Prince of Wales 'all the best with Camilla' was apparently regarded as a security risk and had his name and address taken down by the police. So there were still moments of confusion, and it became abundantly clear in January

1997 that Bolland still had a lot of work to do when, during the Carlton Television monarchy debate, there were those boos whenever anyone said the word 'Camilla', and the studio audience said they would rather have Princess Anne on the throne than Charles. *Harpers & Queen* went out on a limb when they put her at number 47 in a list of 'Women We Love', praising her for her 'strength, humanity and brilliance – she proved it is not only cover girls who capture prince's hearts.' Diana was at the top of the list of 'the ones who let us down'.

Camilla spent the weekend of the monarchy debate with friends around her swimming-pool in the country. She was wearing a flowery bikini – we have the newspaper photographers in the bushes to thank for this nice detail.

St James's Palace announced a five-year strategy aimed at restoring Charles's image in time for the Queen's Golden Jubilee in 2002. Elaine Storkey, a member of the General Synod, warned that an honest approach to the relationship would still not satisfy church leaders. 'Merely spending more time in public with a mistress will solve nothing,' she said.

In August 1996, Andrew Parker Bowles married

Rosemary Pitman. 'She's pretty, chic, well-read and rich,' said a friend. 'She is also lots of fun.' Rosemary Pitman is an old friend of Camilla's. Andrew was in the Horse Guards with her ex-husband. A friend told the press that Camilla felt a bit miserable when Andrew got married – nothing serious, just a bit down in the dumps. A few newspaper diarists then began hinting that she was feeling left out, after Charles took on the even more bouncy and tiggerish Tiggy Legge Bourke as an *über*-nanny/companion for Prince William and Prince Harry. Charles was photographed kissing Tiggy on the cheek on a ski slope, and Camilla was a little put out.

But she had her new house to look forward to. She and Charles had chosen a place called Ray Mill just outside Lacock which is a very pretty National Trust village in Wiltshire. Lacock is where *Middlemarch*, *Pride and Prejudice*, *Moll Flanders* and parts of *Harry Potter* were filmed; there are no satellite dishes but lots of sightseers. Ray Mill House is just outside Lacock, at the back of the village over a humpback bridge – seventeen acres, a swimming-pool, lovely views. Camilla's divorce settlement from Andrew Parker Bowles was £600,000 – not enough to buy a house like Ray

Mill which cost £850,000 – and so there was a lot of media gossip going on about how much the Prince must have contributed.

At one stage Major Shand had plans to move into the barn at Ray Mill but they couldn't get planning permission to turn it into living quarters, so now he lives down in Stourpaine in Dorset with his other daughter, Annabel, instead. A magazine journalist, who visited to write an interiors piece about Annabel Elliot's house, said that the Major was very much in evidence. This was just after there had been some speculation in the newspapers that he had been given rooms in the Robert Kime-refurbished Clarence House and was going to live with Charles and Camilla. He told the journalist that he was keen to be seen by a member of the press at Stourpaine so everyone could see that Annabel hadn't jolly well chucked him out at all!

Camilla moved into Ray Mill in the winter of 1995, and that spring Charles dispatched horse boxes which he had loaded up with his lovingly nurtured plants from Highgrove for her to love and nurture in her new garden. 'It's a cluttered, not very tidy, country home that's full of history and quietness,' says one visitor. She clearly loves it and likes having her own space, even if she spends more and more time at Highgrove. The place will be just what Charles wants a home to be – comfortable, chintzy and a place to squidge about in.' The press nip down occasionally to interview the locals about Camilla. The barmaid in the pub said that she had come across her riding around the lanes. The man standing at the bar shouted, 'In that case, I feel sorry for the horse...'

'All I know', he said, 'is that you never saw a policeman down here before she came. Now the place is crawling with them.' Camilla now has protection – she definitely needs it: she once found a journalist climbing in through her bathroom window. Soon after 11th September 2001, a couple, Reg Spinney and Sheila Muston, were assigned to her. Sheila was used to guarding Prince Harry and Princess Anne. Reg had looked after Prince William. Now they moved into the little cottage on the corner of the drive leading to Camilla's house. The week after Camilla moved in, her closest neighbour received a visit from the royal protection squad. She said she quite understood, and it wasn't at all inconvenient.

The importance of Camilla having her own security was highlighted when, in June 1997, she had a car crash. She was on her way to Highgrove and Caroline Melville Smith, the driver of the other car, said that Camilla was driving 'hellish fast'. Camilla banged her head and hurt her arm and wrist; Caroline Melville Smith suffered some bruises and bewilderment when she looked up and saw Camilla scarpering up a hill. In fact, Camilla was running to get a phone signal. She phoned for the police and an ambulance, before calling Prince Charles, and then, instead of returning to the crash to help the other woman, she stayed put until she was collected by the royal bodyguard, two valets and two other members of Highgrove staff. It wasn't her fault, she wasn't being mean: she couldn't go back in case Caroline Melville Smith was an assassin.

Miss Melville Smith was actually an interior designer. After the crash, her nephew was interviewed by an *Evening Standard* reporter and he described her as a 'terrific extrovert': 'Anyone else would have had a road accident with Johnny Nobody, but she has to have a crash with Camilla Parker Bowles.' Anyone but Camilla would have a crash with Johnny Nobody – she had to have one with a 'terrific extrovert' who had a splendid time telling the press about her brush with Prince Charles's girlfriend. Prince Charles told Camilla she must never drive alone again.

During this period, although it was known that Camilla and Charles were seeing each other, they had yet to be seen together in public. One day in February they both went hunting with the Beaufort – Camilla and her hunter, Molly, went to the meet at 11 am and did the first two hours (no fox), then she left the field and along came Charles (fox up) to finish off the day. So unfair. But being photographed together would be worse. Doing anything together publicly just wasn't worth the risk yet, which meant Camilla had to suffer being recognised in the Glasgow airport branch of Boots while Charles travelled up to Balmoral on one of his mother's aeroplanes. She didn't like it, she never liked being out in public without protection; she got all flustered and worried.

Still, Mark Bolland was busy beavering away at St James's. The fact that Charles and Camilla walked together from the palace to the staff Christmas party at the Ritz that year was Bolland's doing. Camilla, her pashmina blowing in the wind, had that, 'I'm sure you don't really want a picture of me do you?' look about her and walked with small rabbity steps. Certainly, Bolland was doing his best, and he was particularly keen on the idea of Camilla becoming a patron of the National Osteoporosis Society, although it was a risk because charity work was very much Diana's bag.

And so it was that in April 1997 Camilla had a misty, soft-focus official photograph taken and stood in line at a National Osteoporosis Society press conference. Alongside her were other patrons – Claire Rayner, Sir Ranulph Fiennes, the Gold Blend actor Tony Head, Sally Burton, Pat Coombs, Maggie Philbin and Moira Shearer, who is a close friend. Linda Edwards, who became a great friend of Camilla's but died in December 2002 of cancer, was the National Osteoporosis Society director. She said at the time, 'We have benefited from her work over the past two years. She combines energy and enthusiasm with a commitment to challenge the disease which has affected her family so profoundly.' Linda Edwards also said, 'When I asked her to become our director she looked at me very directly and said, "Are you sure it would do you any good?"'

This is probably what Camilla is thinking whenever she faces the photographers although she can on occasions look quite magnificent. On the night of her 50th birthday party at Highgrove, she looked extremely confident and more than ready for her close-up. Prince Charles invited 80 people, Camilla facilitators, including Camilla's father and ex-husband and his new wife Rosemary. The police in the driveway said to the photographers, 'It's a private party but if you want to see the main shot, boys, just stay here.' And then Camilla asked the driver of the Ford Mondeo she arrived in to slow down so they could all have a really good look at the new necklace Charles had bought her for her birthday.

Jilly Cooper was there in the 120ft marquee listening to the clarinetist and the Welsh harpist, and Melvyn Bragg and dear old Nicholas Soames. So much had changed, new house, new birthday necklace from the Prince, everyone newly divorced, new clothes, new spin doctor, a positive result from a MORI Poll in the *Mail on Sunday*, and the Princess of Wales out of the country on holiday with Dodi Fayed.

Chapter Fifteen

There were some who would later say that
Diana, Princess of Wales, went away just
because she didn't want to be around on Camilla's
big birthday night. It is unlikely that this is true
because, regardless of any parties going on at
Highgrove, it was the summer, it was the school
holidays and it was Diana's turn to have the boys
for a while – so of course she went away.

Camilla looked lovely at her party, wearing a
dark, sleeveless silk dress and the flower-link diamond necklace from Charles, but Diana looked
sexier on the beach. And, as the summer went on,
and Camilla flew to Malaga on her way to stay
with the Marquess and Marchioness of Douro –
prompting a few lines in the papers about the
fact that she flew from Stansted on a £145 charter

flight – so Diana filled the front pages from France in her leopard-print swimsuit. Every day she was in the papers; she was so glamorous by now in her new royal-free life. She looked amazing, Amazonian and fit and incredibly beautiful.

Her friend Gianni Versace had been murdered just a few weeks earlier and Diana had been photographed with people like Elton John and Donatella Versace and Mario Testino. Then there she was in the sun on a jet-ski, all blonde and suntan. After the boys had been brought back to England to be with their shooting and fishing father, after a restful, restorative holiday with her best friend Rosa Monckton, Diana returned to France to be with Dodi, her new, rich, high-living love interest.

It was Diana's summer. She had set the tone that August, monopolized the newspapers, kept us intrigued and enthralled. And then it all ended – suddenly, and so desperately shockingly, in a high-speed car chase.

It took a while after the shock of Diana's death for the papers to turn to Camilla and for the pundits to work out that she and the Prince were back to square one. In fact they were back at square minus ten. The Royals were looking pretty awful to most of the people after the Queen's reluctance to lower a flag over Diana's funeral, and Earl Spencer's address about the boys and blood family. And Camilla, holed up at Ray Mill, was looking like the old trout again, the haddock, the horse, the wicked witch of the west, the wife-stealer. There was the inevitable Camilla backlash; nothing too great because, for months and months to come, the papers and the people would still be preoccupied with the death of Diana. But those small end-columns at the end of bigger columns carried Camilla snipes – she was manipulative, she had known all along that she would become his permanent mistress, she was driven by ambition, she made him think it was alright to have a wife and a mistress because that is what his great, great grandfather had done.

Any progress Camilla had made, any thread of normality running through her life, her routine between Ray Mill and Highgrove and St James's dissolved. She moved her belongings out of Highgrove. It was crucial that to the outside world she was living the quiet life of a recently divorced, unattached woman.

Camilla said that her first thought on hearing of Diana's death was for the boys, and, much as people might have disliked her, nobody would disbelieve that from Camilla the mother.

The Bolland spinning had to stop, of course, the moment Diana died. An evening 'of enchantment, fascination, and the unexpected', in aid of the National Osteoporosis Society which was to have been Camilla's first big step out in public, was cancelled.

It was six months before she went anywhere other than Highgrove again. Someone who knows her well says that she was used to not venturing far from home, except when on holiday. In fact after 1992, the *annus horribilis*, it was ten years before she set foot in a London restaurant.

In May 1998 she went to her godson Henry Dent Brocklehurst's wedding and she got herself in the papers for it because it was a high-profile affair – Mick Jagger was there, as well as Hugh Grant and Claudia Schiffer.

By July, though, the spinners and the leakers were back in action and on 9th July the *Sun* ran a 'world exclusive' headlined 'Camilla meets Wills'. Prince William, so the story went, had told his father that he would be stopping off briefly at St James's Palace to change his clothes before going out again. Prince Charles told Prince William that it was likely that Mrs Parker Bowles would be around and that it was up to him whether or not he would like to meet her, and William said he would. So they were introduced to each other and sat about on sofas having a chat and drinking fruit juice until it was time for William to go.

Some would have it that the only reason the Princes had never met their father's 'friend' before was that Tiggy Legge Bourke, their bouncy Tiggerish nanny/companion, had a sharp streak of jealousy running through her, had always had a bit more than a soft spot for Prince Charles herself and had, up until this point, managed to engineer the Princes' lives so they never encountered Mrs Parker Bowles.

What gave the story of William's eventual meeting with Camilla some authenticity was a very Camilla-ish detail. Immediately after William had gone, she is said to have declared breathily, 'I really need a gin and tonic.' There was a great deal of clamour in the press about this story, more about how the story came to find its way into the *Sun* than about the significance of Prince William meeting his father's girlfriend just six months after Diana's death. What they were all het up about was the suspicion that Mark Bolland had 'leaked' the story, that Prince William was being bartered in the Camilla campaign. Some thought that the story might have come from Peter Mandelson, the Labour MP who at that time was still Minister without Portfolio, about to be made Trade and Industry Secretary, and who was one of Camilla's new best friends – she had been bending his ear over the proposed fox-hunting ban.

In the end, the person who took the rap was Camilla's 42-year-old personal assistant, Amanda MacManus, who was married to James MacManus, managing editor of *Times* supplements. Mrs MacManus had told Mr MacManus in secret and Mr MacManus had told another newspaper executive who then told someone at the *Sun* who had no intention of staying shtum with such a lovely story. Amanda MacManus resigned, saying she was very sorry and particularly sad to be leaving such a 'remarkable employer', and Camilla made it clear that she was really very upset. She was so upset that Amanda MacManus was reinstated within a year. Since then, due to financial cut-backs, controversy, personal reasons or whatever, Mrs MacManus and Camilla have had a pretty on-off relationship. Whether she is or isn't in the employ of St Jamess Palace, or

Clarence House, as Prince Charles's court is now known, is anyone's guess.

It was an intriguing episode for those who knew little of the way Camilla Parker Bowles was now leading her life. Suddenly we knew that she had such a thing as a personal assistant, and that she really did inhabit St James's Palace. Three days before the *Sun* scoop, the *Sunday Mirror* ran a three-page story about a surprise party which Prince Harry and Prince William were organizing for their father's 50th birthday. The result was that it was no longer a surprise. The Princes were furious and the palace demanded an apology which they got.

The party went ahead and Camilla, because she had now met Prince William and apparently Prince Harry (another *Sun* scoop), at a Highgrove tea party, was allowed to be invited. It was an advance birthday party – well ahead of Prince Charles's actual birthday in November and it took the form of an hour-long comedy revue performed by Emma Thompson, Stephen Fry and Rowan Atkinson.

William and Harry and Charles had a feel-good feeling about them now and, although Camilla was trailing quite a long way behind, she wasn't receiving hate-mail any more. There was a wobbly moment ,when it looked as if she was going to drop back a bit, after Penny Junor published a 50th-birthday biography of the Prince, in which she accused Diana of being the first to commit adultery – with her bodyguard Barry Mannakee. Junor also said that Diana was responsible for the Camillagate tapes and that she had sometimes phoned Camilla in the night to tell her she had hired a hit-man and that he was in the garden waiting to kill her.

No one was ready for bad things to be said about Diana and as usual it rebounded on Camilla. But a measure of how things had moved on was that, on this occasion, the Prince and Mrs Parker Bowles issued a joint statement in which they distanced themselves from the book. There was still an almighty row, because it turned out that Penny Junor had spoken to friends, relatives and employees of the Prince, although none of them later admitted saying anything about Diana or about Charles or Camilla's personal life. When asked if she had helped Junor with the book, Linda Edwards of the National Osteoporosis Society said, 'We talked about Camilla Parker Bowles's relationship with the charity. I did not speak about her relationship with Prince Charles. It is a sadness that the public has not been able to see Camilla as we have seen her – a warm, sincere, friendly woman. She has been misrepresented and I can't help but hope that out of all this current controversy a kinder picture will emerge of Camilla.'

Few people took any notice of Penny Junor's stories about Diana, although presumably the author thought they were true or she wouldn't have published them. But the media were still making a fuss over who Junor could possibly have spoken to and one newspaper came to the conclusion that 'the Prince now has a dangerously hyperactive alternative court around him.'

It was true, and within the next few years, significantly in the aftermath of the Paul Burrell trial in 2003, and, later that year, in the Paul Burrell biography, it would become clear quite how controlling and complex that court was. Camilla's life was so much more complicated now. Those days when she had had to worry about safehouses and grabbing a night here and night there with Prince Charles were over. Now she could be with him any time she wanted. The problem was making the public see that it was all right for them to be together any time they wanted.

They weren't looking quite so like the middle-aged couple who enjoyed a bit of gardening and a spot of painting any more. They were being spun and manipulated, quite willingly apparently, and this spinning reached something of a climax in January 1999 when they appeared on the steps of the Ritz Hotel in Piccadilly together.

The press had been feeling miffed because whenever Prince Charles and Camilla went out to a wedding or a dinner or to the theatre, or a function, they arrived and left separately and they made sure they kept their distance so that they never appeared alongside each other in the same photograph.

It was said that a photograph of the two of them – a clear photo, not an out-of-focus, snatched one – preferably touching each other, would be worth millions. So the reasons behind the tip off which led to over 200 photographers waiting outside the Ritz that January night were three-fold. One, it would be a major step forward in the Camilla campaign; two, it would immediately stop the chase – the picture would be in the bag, the world would have seen Charles and Camilla together – and three, it wasn't long until

Prince Edward's wedding to Sophie Rhys Jones, and it would be really nice if Camilla could go without attracting too much attention away from those getting married.

The event at the Ritz was Camilla's sister's 50th birthday party and the press had been tipped off that Charles and Camilla would leave together. Camilla arrived at 8.45pm in a black Tomasz Starzewski dress and a Ford Mondeo driven by an ex-royal protection squad officer. She had Tom and Laura with her. In the lobby of the hotel a pianist was playing 'Woman in Love'. The Prince who was busy having his own dinner party at St James's didn't turn up until eleven. The newspaper reports the following day said that Camilla drank Martini, then stuck to water because she wanted her wits about her. She had a heavy cold and there is no question she was dreading the fifteen seconds of flashbulbs about to be blown in her face.

Someone described it as one of the greatest pictures in history. In fact it was of two middle-aged people making their way down a set of hotel steps and into a car. Camilla walked slightly behind Charles looking terrified. The next day, although the moment made it on to the lunchtime television news bulletins, it then had to be pulled in case the flashes sparked seizures in epileptics – only three flashes of light per second are allowed. When Camilla and Charles walked, not even arm in arm, out of the Ritz, there were nine camera flashes per second. You could see it from space. It was just eighteen months since Diana had died.

When Charles woke up the next morning, and heard his short walk with Camilla being dissected on Radio Four, he turned off his bedside radio.

But still the polls failed to deliver on Mrs Parker Bowles – the people thought it looked like she was enjoying all the privileges without having to open a single fête.

**

'Coming-out liberated Camilla,' says a close friend. And it was true. They went to the theatre together, they went to dinner at friends' houses together. Camilla would sometimes even have her very own public engagements. In June 1999 she was accompanied by Bolland and a bodyguard when she visited 'The Young Artists of the Future Show' at a Sue Ryder home in Cheltenham. She was particularly impressed by the cat-themed clay and stone sculpture of eighteen-year-old

Cirencester college student George Henriques. 'It was a proud moment for me when Camilla said she liked my work,' said the GNVQ advanced art and design student.

Then some property developers in Chiswick, West London, wanted to call a block of flats which had been built on the site of an old carpet warehouse 'Camilla House'. The local Tory councillor, Peter Thompson, said, 'The developers must be living in cloud-cuckoo-land if they think that anyone will want to buy a property with such a cheap and offensive name.' In November, a painting of Camilla was stolen from a Scottish art gallery. It was hand-crafted and only four inches high. The owner, Frank Manclark, took 80 hours to create an exact image of Mrs Parker Bowles. He was planning to enter it at the world exhibition of miniature art held in Tasmania.

That summer Camilla smartened herself up. She wore Valentino to a dinner held by a Greek shipping tycoon, Theodore Angelopoulos, in aid of the Prince's architectural and environment foundation. Valentino was there and he said he was delighted that Mrs Parker Bowles was wearing one of his dresses and that she looked elegant in her matching pashmina and diamond necklace.

The previous year she had been called 'The Queen of Frump – the biggest bomb to hit Britain since the Blitz' by Richard Blackwell, the author of the America's best and worst dressed lists.

Camilla is, even these days, not an international shopper. She doesn't go to the collections, she doesn't make appointments to visit Prada or Gucci early in the morning or late at night with a personal stylist which is how a real queen or princess would shop. Camilla's favourite outlet was for many years a small boutique in Hungerford. Her shopping list would have read: new trug basket, some twine, a pound of chipolatas and four new dresses for Ascot week.

The owner of the boutique in Hungerford, which was called Jeanne Petitt, would have Camilla firmly fixed in her mind when she went to the collections and she would buy in things she thought would particularly suit. Camilla was especially keen on Tomasz Starzewski, who, interestingly, was a favourite of the Princess of Wales. 'I was impressed,' Starzewski says, 'by the fact that when the Princess of Wales was alive and Camilla was wanting to wear my clothes she had the integrity to go about it in a tactful way. She did not wish to compete, or be photographed competing, with Diana. Châpeau off to her.'

But it wasn't châpeau off to Camilla when she decided to venture way, way beyond Hungerford to Paris to see a Stella McCartney for Chloë fashion show. It was a mystery why she did it, not only to the fashion editors who suddenly had themselves a story to tell, but to Stella McCartney, the vegetarian, anti-fur, daughter of Linda, scion of the tofu-burger empire, herself.

'Oh My God, Camilla's here,' is what she said when she peeked out from behind the catwalk and saw the queen of the fox-hunt sitting there in her front-row seat.

Camilla was, by now, surrounded by photographers. This is what happens at fashion shows: a famous person arrives; the catwalk photographers stampede and the designer has guaranteed coverage in the following days' papers. But who had invited Camilla?

It was Lord Douro, the man with the bolthole in Spain, the son of the Duke of Wellington who was also a board member at the Vendôme Luxury Group which owned the Chloë label. 'If only we had known she was coming,' said a PR, 'we could have arranged better security. It's a nightmare, what with having to provide cover for Sir Paul

McCartney as well.' Mick Hucknall of Simply Red was there, too.

Camilla, it turned out, had gone to Paris – on a Dunhill (also owned by Vendôme) private jet, for a short break. She had lunch, then dinner, then went to Stella McCartney's show. She thought, presumably, that it would be a bit of a jolly, a night out with friends. But she caused a terrific rumpus and not just because of McCartney's anti-blood sport feelings, but also because at Chloë the models are mostly wearing hipsters and Camilla may have an inner something but she just isn't built for hipsters. Mounir Mouffaridge who is the president of Chloë said that Mrs Parker Bowles was carrying a Chloë handbag, but it wouldn't have been a leather one.

The Stella McCartney incident aside, there really was very little the fashion writers could say about Camilla, so they concentrated on the little details. In May 1999, she hosted a dinner at the Ritz to thank supporters of the National Osteoporosis Society, and she had pinned to her short, black dress a gold, silver and enamel brooch in the shape of the Prince of Wales feathers.

It was a present from Prince Charles and he has given the same thing to six other women – Lady

Susan Hussey, a senior lady-in-waiting to the Queen who is William's godmother, Patty Palmer-Tomkinson, Emilie van Cutsem, Julia Cleverdon who works for one of the Prince's charities and Fiona Shackleton, his lawyer. Camilla also has a black pearl and diamond fleur-de-lys brooch, another present from Charles, which is unique and was originally a gift from Edward VII to Mrs Keppel.

Generally what fashion reports there were were good – a cream suit here, a little black dress there, with the occasional 'must try harder' when it didn't look as if she had made the effort. Camilla never went over the top; she never got carried away. Her clothes were simple and respectable with the occasional low décolleté or discreet slit up the side of a skirt. There have been forays in to big hats, but Camilla, like the Queen, is not very tall and can't really carry them off. One friend of hers maintains that the only mistake Camilla has ever really made in her life was a cartwheel hat she once wore to a wedding: 'She really mustn't do cartwheels.'

Meanwhile, in Australia a report from the Paris collections warned that Chanel's tweedy tailoring was best carried off with jeans, not gumboots in order to escape the 'Camilla Parker Bowles comparison'. But this idea of Camilla is out of date. By 2003 people were commenting not so much on her country tweediness as her '*Hello!* Magazine hair-do's'. He regular trips to the colourist, Jo Hansford, in Mayfair mean that, as one newspaper diarist put it, 'her hair is now so blonde she could qualify for sponsorship from the peroxide industry'. And there have also been reports that she employs the same hairdresser as Joan Collins; a chap called Hugh Green who charges £250 a time.

The New York fashion designer Oscar de la Renta, who dresses Manhattan socialites and presidents' wives, and who met Camilla in September 1999, said, when asked if Camilla should have a makeover: 'To me Camilla is the epitome of country style. When we met I didn't notice what she was wearing and that is the mark of a truly fashionable woman, and,' he sighed with relief, 'she didn't utter a word about fashion. I would be delighted if Camilla was given lots of de la Renta dresses, but she really doesn't need them because she has her own style. Those with real style understand they don't have to be fashion victims. When I think of an English woman, I think of a woman tending a beautiful rose garden and when I think of an American I think of her going to work, all tense and ambitious. On a woman as confident about herself as Camilla, some of my expensive clothes, however, would look very beautiful, very feminine.' He was hedging his bets probably, because he wasn't quite sure if it would be a good thing or a bad thing to dress Camilla Parker Bowles – good PR or bad PR. Would future Hollywood film actors want to wear the same designer label as Mrs Parker Bowles, mother of two, from Wiltshire?

Indeed four years later the American fashion fraternity was not being so generous about Camilla's wardrobe and one pundit described the outfits she wore on a trip to New York in 1999 as 'a profusion of badly fitting pink'.

***

Camilla met Oscar in Manhattan in September 1999. She was on a four-day trip, an official coming-out in America, a royal tour without a proper royal. It was Mark Bolland's idea. Bolland went with her, so did the reinstated Amanda McManus – they flew Concorde, paid for by Prince Charles.

They were met by Michael Fawcett, a former valet to Charles, someone who was described as a major figure in the domestic circle who had done an advance recce.

But, even with all this support, Camilla was in dangerous territory – this was Diana-land. She stayed at Diana's New York hotel, the Carlyle. 'She had to be really persuaded to go,' says a close friend. 'It was the most terrifying experience of her life. She knew that in New York they were just so pro-Diana. She didn't think she was beautiful enough. She didn't think it was her world; her world is upper-class balls at home. She reads everything that is written about her and it does hurt her, although she is tougher these days. But in New York Anna Wintour [British-born editor of *American Vogue*] took her on board and fell for her and made it easier.'

In fact, the only thing they didn't like about Camilla in Manhattan was her voice, her deep, drawly voice. 'You see, Diana's voice was so soft and gentle,' said Camilla's friend.

In America, though, they love British royalty and Camilla came pretty close. The society mavens of the East Coast really wanted to meet her at Brooke Astor's lunch in Park Avenue –

Catherine Zeta Jones and Michael Douglas were invited. When Brooke Astor was a child she had met Alice Keppel and all those years later, in her toast to Mrs Keppel's great-granddaughter, she said that Camilla had done very well by her great-grandmother and everybody laughed.

Kofi Annan was there with his wife Nane Lagergren, who is a lawyer. Mort Zuckerman the publisher was there and so was Michael Bloomberg the financier and Vartan Gregorian the head of the Carnegie Corporation.

The mavens also wanted to be invited along when Camilla visited Scott Bessent, a rich financier with a house in East Hampton called Southern Dunes. Camilla went body-surfing, dined with the Bessents at local restaurants and visited a friend of a friend's mysterious and beautiful wilderness garden.

Eileen Guggenheim, who is married to Russell Wilkinson of Wilkinson Sword fame, took Camilla to the New York Academy of Art and they stopped for lunch at Mercer's Kitchen, which is where people like Gwyneth Paltrow and Nicole Kidman eat. Camilla went to a party for Robert Kime, her interior designer, and there was a security scare when a man claimed to have planted explosives in front of the venue on Third Avenue – so really her trip had all the fine details of a good royal tour.

The verdict was that Camilla was amusing and chatty. 'We've been singing her praises,' said someone who met her. 'It was made clear to us at Brooke Astor's lunch that we were lunching with the mistress of the Prince of Wales and we loved it. There was a refreshing candour.' But she didn't dazzle like the silky-skinned Diana had.

Charles, meanwhile, was on holiday in Scotland with his grandmother.

Chapter Sixteen

Camilla's New York trip was a PR exercise. At the time it was described as 'a family holiday to see old friends', but nobody was fooled, and it is now admitted that it was 100 per cent pure PR, not just for Camilla and Charles, 'the acceptable couple', but also for Charles's charities, to which a lot of wealthy, high-profile Americans contribute a great deal of money. It worked quite well and, by the time Charles and Camilla moved into Clarence House together in 2003, she was able to play hostess at the extravagant dinners given for those wealthy, high-profile Americans and no eyebrows were raised. It showed everyone that Camilla could do the royal thing. In fact, she could do more than that. Camilla is too clever to just make casual nice-nice with people – she entertains and amuses them, makes wry jokes, uses irony. The New York experience not only showed that Camilla was all right to go out in public, was reasonably good at schmoozing, it also pointed to the future – that this is what Camilla might do: act as a representative for Prince Charles's charities and projects. Except that someone who knows her well says, 'She is lazy. She is a lazy woman, she certainly doesn't want to work. Charles and Camilla argue about how little she really wants to get involved.'

Perhaps, then, things have changed since the Camillagate tape. Perhaps these days Camilla is not so keen to read his speeches. A St James's Palace aide once said that Camilla was happy with her relationship with the Prince of Wales 'because she cannot stand the thought of being ordered to take a more prominent role in public life'. But this is wrong too because Camilla gets upset if she is not included often enough in Prince Charles's working life and if the courtiers feel that there are times when she really should take a back seat; times when Charles is on the ropes because of yet another scandal, usually emerging from beyond his wife's grave... That is when Camilla retires hurt to the country, only these days she puts on gloves before weeding around the taddle stones.

Back in the late 1990s, though, she was happy just to do the partying, particularly with the Americans. At that time, when every Camilla 'first' was being reported in the papers and on the evening news, it was noted that she had, for the 'first' time, attended a function at Buckingham Palace for some visiting Americans – all high-profile names, all with big wallets, all worthwhile benefactors of Prince Charles's charities.

The dinner was for 80 and it should have been held at Hampton Court Palace, but someone forgot to book it so the Queen let them use her palace instead. The Prince told his guests that it was not often he was granted this privilege. 'When the cat is away,' he said, 'the mice will play.' Which made them all chortle.

Another one of these Buckingham Palace dinners, in 2001, was photographed by *Vanity Fair*, which meant that the folks back home could witness Lily Safra, Betsey Bloomingdale, Blaine Trump, Joan Rivers, Patty Hearst and other wealthy charity patrons being entertained by 'The Prince of Wales of England', as a royal memorabilia collector in the USA once described him.

Camilla was there, once again, at the palace as co-host, right across the centre spread of *Vanity Fair*. So it was all very open, out there in the public domain. Everyone knew, everyone could see them together and most people thought it was all right, although they weren't so sure about a marriage and they were definitely not sure about a future Queen Camilla.

Sometimes the pro-Camilla spinning spun out of control and the Queen pursed her lips in anger, because it was setting St James's Palace and Buckingham Palace press offices against each other. Charles's lot were dissing the other lot to make themselves look good by comparison.

The Queen doesn't dislike Camilla. She has nothing against her personally; in fact a close friend of Camilla's says that the Queen is rather fond of her and it's Charles she has a problem with – his dithering, his bad decisions, the mess he has made of everything. But, of course, the Queen can't publicly be seen to be liking Camilla or enjoying her company, so she is careful to avoid this. The result is that whenever there is a chance of them meeting, or a rumour that they have spent any time whatsoever in the same building, or even on the same racecourse as each other, the royal watchers start speculating away.

Camilla wasn't in the end invited to the Earl and Countess of Wessex's wedding. It would have caused too much of a media fuss. And, when Prince Charles threw a party for his friend, the exiled King Constantine of Greece's 60th birthday, the Queen was in a terrible dither about whether she should or shouldn't go. Finally, after Charles put a lot of pressure on her, the Queen decided that she would go and the next day the papers were full of Camilla's curtsey, how long the Queen spent talking to Camilla, how long the Queen spent not talking to Camilla, and what it all meant for the future of the monarchy.

Then there was Prince Charles's 50th birthday in 1998. First, there was the party that Prince William and Prince Harry organized. Camilla was allowed to go to that one because she had already met Prince William and Prince Harry and the Queen wasn't going to be there anyway. Then, in November, there was the big party which Camilla hosted at Highgrove. The Queen and Prince Phillip didn't go; they looked the other way and spent that night at Sandringham.

Camilla was driven into Highgrove in a royal car, her sister Annabel was with her and for the second time she slowed down for the photographers. She was wearing an Alice Keppel diamond necklace and an emerald-green velvet dress. That week the Bishop of Durham said it would be 'more desirable morally' for Prince Charles and Camilla to marry, which was helpful but made no difference.

The Queen stood firm, however, and Camilla was not invited to the official 50th birthday reception at Buckingham Palace.

There were tantrums and flounces, too, between Prince Charles and his mother over the party held at Windsor in June 2000. It was a multi-purpose party – to celebrate the Queen Mother's 100th birthday, Princess Margaret's 70th, Princess Anne's 50th, Prince Andrew's 40th and Prince William's 18th. Charles threatened to boycott it unless Camilla could go.

It must have seemed especially unfair that Andrew Parker Bowles was allowed to go because he was such a good friend of the Queen Mother's. But the Queen would not relent and so Charles, who had no choice but to turn up, went, sulked and left early. He is said to alternate between rage and deep depression when it comes to the Queen's attitude towards his non-negotiable Camilla.

By the time the Queen's Golden Jubilee came round in 2002 the royal correspondents were self-combusting with the news that Mrs Parker Bowles had been invited to sit up with the rest of the family, just one row behind Her Majesty, during a classical music concert at Buckingham Palace. She wore a crisp pale-pink suit and cream court shoes.

A close friend of Camilla's tells a story which says a lot about the relationship between her and the Queen. It was Christmas 2002 and Camilla had asked her best friend Patty Palmer-Tomkinson to go with her to her staff party at Axis, the restaurant at No 1 The Aldwych. Mrs Palmer-Tomkinson was asked to arrive at St James's Palace precisely on time – which she duly did. The two women then got into an official car, complete with an aide – probably Mark Bolland – a police-woman and a chauffeur.

Mrs Palmer-Tomkinson was surprised that Camilla had her own policewoman and said something along the lines of 'Blimey, Camilla, you've got grand.' Then, as they pulled out into the Mall, Mrs Palmer-Tomkinson spotted some police outriders and was even more surprised, saying something like 'Goodness gracious, Camilla, you've even got outriders!'

'No,' said Camilla, 'They're not for me. They're for"Mummy".'

'Mummy' of course was the Queen – it's what Prince Charles calls her, as we found out when the Queen toasted her son on his 50th birthday and he thanked her and called her 'Mummy'.

Camilla then proceeded to hang out of the car window, craning her neck for a look at 'Mummy', and fretting over whether 'Mummy' might be going to No 1 The Aldwych, too, and whether the Queen had spotted her hanging out of the car window.

**

The public interest in Camilla was by now dwindling – she didn't dazzle, she didn't have silky skin, she seemed perfectly nice but she wasn't a secret any more and she had won over the press with her Enid Blyton personality, smiling at them from horseback, waving at them in country lanes and chattily acknowledging them when she accompanied Prince Charles on official engagements – when she would walk several paces behind him.

People weren't that interested in turning out to see her any more or turning the page to see her or turning on the television to see her. The press caught her occasionally but the stories they published were not really about her. They were about whether or not she and Prince Charles would ever marry; would she, could she become queen; and what did his mother think of it all.

And now Camilla was enjoying herself. A friend of hers says she loves 'the hairdressers and the jewels'. She is still happy to work herself into a muck sweat with the Beaufort and then, after a quick swipe with a wet flannel, jump into a ball gown – if she has the chance.

But her life has changed. When she goes out now she goes to grand and expensive parties where the women wear Gucci and Armani. She goes to fashion parties and wears Anthony Price and Valentino and Versace – it was the Prince who chose the Versace dress she wore to the Prince's Trust foundation dinner in 2000. She sat next to David Coulthard and Harry Oppenheimer; Lauren Bacall was there and Mary Lou Vanderbilt. Alan Whicker was there with his partner Valerie Kleeman who used to be in the same lacrosse team as Camilla at Queen's Gate, which proves she definitely does have input into the guest list because there is no earthly reason why Alan

Whicker should have been there otherwise. Even Prince Charles had to ask him what he was doing there.

Michael Fawcett, Prince Charles's indispensable former valet, designed the table decorations for this event. They were very creative and interesting: white roses, cactus and silver-sprayed moss enclosed in a swirl of barbed wire.

These days Camilla doesn't French-kiss on the dance floor at polo balls; she sits down to eat with the Editor of *Vogue*, with Elton John and David Furnish. She is there at Sandringham with the Prince every March when he invites people from the 'arts' for the weekend and conducts them on tours of ecclesiastical architecture. So she mixes with actors and artists. She invites Barbara Windsor to her parties because she loves *EastEnders* (she was especially gripped by the return of Dirty Den in October 2003 – light relief from the Burrell revelations of that time which were threatening to send her scurrying back to the country) and Barbara Windsor pitches up because Camilla is tremendous fun, and wouldn't we all if we had an invite from the Prince of Wales's girlfriend?

In August, Camilla and Charles went on a

Mediterranean cruise with William, Harry, some Van Cutsems, some of William and Harry's cousins, Charles's old nanny Mabel Anderson, some Palmer-Tomkinsons and assorted other dear friends.

Every so often an outboard motor full of photographers would chug into view, and one day some Greek Cypriot activists interrupted Prince Charles's morning swim by threatening him with a harpoon and telling him they were going to murder his mother.

They were seen off by security, and Charles and Camilla were briefly reminded that their lives were not all fun and messing about on boats and never could be. But there was now a sense of normality about them: they were a couple, holidaying with friends and family – people who understood their need to be together.

In June 1999, Charles and Camilla went to stay with the Douros again, in Spain. They were seen 'riding in the foothills', in the early evening sun. What a life.

'Camilla is having a great time,' says someone who knows them both well. 'She goes to good parties. She spent 20 years being in the country with a boring adulterer and, relatively, compared to others in their social circles, she and Andrew didn't have much money. Now she loves going off in John Latsis's yacht. And think about it, Charles has an income of seven million a year.'

There have been some difficult moments along the way that were made more difficult by the newspapers – for instance the 'Tom takes cocaine' story in which a reporter tricked Tom Parker Bowles into telling her where, at the Cannes Film festival in May 1999, she could get some cocaine.

As Derek Davison, who is a partner in the film publicity agency for which Tom was working, said, drug-taking 'is part of our life in general'. He was speaking the truth. Cocaine in those circles is not a story – the story was only a story because it was about the son of the Prince of Wales's girl-friend. In any other circumstances it would have only made the papers if it had been about some-one working in the film industry who didn't know how to get hold of cocaine in Cannes.

But Tom Parker Bowles, it was revealed, had earlier been cautioned for possession of ecstasy and cannabis and, most important of all, he was known to be close to Prince William. The *People* newspaper reported: '... shocked Camilla broke down weeping as she blamed herself.

Heartbreakingly, she asked her son "Why? Where did we go wrong... are you hooked, son?" There was nothing Charles could say to her. He just held her in his arms as she sobbed.'

Of course, nobody actually knows if Camilla sobbed or if she called Tom 'son', or if Charles held her in his arms, although he did let it be known that he had read Tom the riot act and of course it was distressing and upsetting for both of Tom's parents.

And it was very important that, for the benefit of the outside world, they were seen to be angry and upset. How they were seen to behave was very important in the Mark Bolland-led campaign to promote Camilla.

'The big issue is travelling,' says a friend, 'Charles will never let her travel at public expense. Only in cars which are funded by Duchy money. They know that the people of this country tolerate her, but that it could change. Charles and Camilla will not be hostage to fortune. This is why they never fly together. She always goes commercial on British Airways. They have an arrangement with British airways so that she always goes in the VIP room for security reasons and because she hates being stared at. The one thing she regrets about her life now is the loss of anonymity.'

When Camilla tags along on official engage-ments, she has to be seen to be walking behind Charles. She can't be seen to be being treated like a royal; she mustn't look as if she has been funded by the tax payer. And on the few occasions when she has, or when others have singled her out from your average common or garden private citizen, the press have spat and bristled – they don't like it.

On 13th September 2001, when Camilla visited the American Embassy in Grosvenor Square to write a message in the book of condolence for the victims of 9/11, she was, reported the *Daily Mail*, 'received in the style of a senior politician'.

A spokesman for the embassy said she could not comment on what the *Daily Mail* described as a 'breach of etiquette', but confirmed that Mrs Parker Bowles had received 'exactly the same treatment' as Baroness Thatcher and William Hague who was at the time the leader of the Conservative party. Meanwhile, Ken Livingstone, the Mayor of London, was left to wander around Grosvenor Square unescorted.

'Of course, Mrs Parker Bowles is viewed as a private individual, but she is an extremely famous private individual and there was no possibility of us leaving her by herself among the crowds and the cameras,' said the spokesman.

And then a few months later came the telling squabble, which followed the opening of an exhibition of royal tiaras at the Victoria & Albert Museum. The 82-year-old Duchess of Devonshire, provider of a safe-house down the years, most beloved granny figure to the Prince of Wales, was apparently most put out when Camilla was given an escorted preview of the exhibition. As Mrs Parker Bowles was being shown around, a gentle and courteous hand at her back to guide her, others – titled others, some of whom had even lent their very own tiaras for the exhibition, an assortment of dukes, duchesses, viscounts and princes – were made to wait in an anteroom.

'I suppose she is surveying her kingdom,' is what the Duchess of Devonshire allegedly said about Camilla's private view, although she later hotly denied that she had said any such thing. 'Pure invention,' she barked, 'Camilla and I are very old friends.'

The papers loved this little spat and columnists wondered whether Camilla was turning grand.

One of the Alice Keppel keepsakes which

Charles bought for Camilla used to be a tiara, but he had it turned into a necklace for her. 'It is probably not a good idea for Camilla to start wearing tiaras rather grandly; people might get the wrong idea,' said a friend.

Chapter Seventeen

These days Camilla isn't really regarded as a private citizen and, even if she doesn't mean to behave grandly, she is treated as if she is grand. People bow and scrape because she is famous. They bow and scrape for Camilla Parker Bowles just as they do for daytime television presenters. She is treated like a celebrity but not quite like royalty, because whereas she might be asked by the local car wash to sign a photograph of herself – 'A right royal Car Wash – My favourite!' – Prince Charles would not. Neither would the Queen, although Princess Michael of Kent might.

Camilla attends official engagements with Prince Charles so regularly now that nobody says anything about it any more, although when Bolland finally left and Sir Michael Peat took over there was an attempt to make Camilla stay at home. Whether she is allowed to go or not very much depends on the Prince's profile at any given moment. If the country is pleased with him he can have Camilla by his side and the theory is we will love her because we love him. If he is in our bad books we do not want him compounding his offences by parading his mistress for all to see.

It was interesting that when, on one of the occasions she did accompany him on an official visit, and her body language was analysed for a television documentary – it was found to be almost identical to her Prince's; he and she were synchronised, even though they couldn't see each other – same hand up to face followed by hand down to pocket, same pinching fingers at the edge of their jackets, same twiddling the pinky ring. They were as one.

At the close of the day nobody now flinches when Camilla and Charles climb into the same car together and head off home like an old married couple to a night in with *The Weakest Link* and *The Royle Family*. There is barely a murmur from the press these days when Camilla is included in private family events, although occasions such as her first inclusion at a Balmoral barbecue

(October 2003) are still noted for delectation and analysis.

Aaron Barschak, who dressed as Osama bin Laden in a pink dress, then gatecrashed Prince William's 21st birthday party at Windsor in June 2003, says the question he is asked the most about his stunt is 'What was Camilla Parker Bowles like?' People don't ask him if she was there; they take it for granted she was there.

But they do want to know what she is like. She has rarely spoken in public, so we don't know her speech inflections or timing and there is little for us or the impersonators to go on. Once, in Lisbon, at a National Osteoporosis seminar, Camilla gave a speech and we heard her talking, but she wasn't being herself, her nerves wouldn't allow her inner something to glow through. She was dressed in a mother-of-the-bride-ish pale blue suit and had been put next to the cool and beautiful Queen Rania of Jordan.

She was less embarrassed and more forthright on another occasion, when she was stopped by a television news reporter on her way into a function to promote a leaflet about osteoporosis. She held the leaflet up and, while she talked urgently about what an important leaflet it was, she shook it at the reporter like a terrier shaking a rat.

Just as with any other celebrity, if Camilla ever speaks to members of the public they remember her words and repeat them for the rest of their lives in their story of the time they met Camilla Parker Bowles.

'It was a tremendous honour to have her in my home,' said Mrs Catherine Stephens of Newcastle, after Camilla had paid her a visit and had a cup of tea.

In July 2003 at the 122nd Sandringham Flower Show, Dorothy Edwards, aged 77, ducked under a rope to shake Camilla's hand and then wouldn't let go because she just couldn't stop herself from kissing it. Mrs Edwards said later that she was shaking with excitement.

Not everyone has quite such intense feelings for Camilla. Meat Loaf, the lead singer of the rock band Bat Out of Hell, said, at the prospect of meeting her after a concert in Hyde Park, 'Camilla – she's not a royal, is she? She's the mistress.' And when Sharon Osbourne, the wife of Ozzie, met the mistress at the Golden Jubilee pop concert at Buckingham Palace she is reported to have walked up to Camilla, reached out with both hands, and squeezed her breasts. 'You've got gorgeous old

tits,' she said. Camilla apparently smiled and nodded in response which is probably what she did
two and half decades ago when Charles couldn't
help plunging his hands into her cleavage.

When she went to the tenth anniversary party
of the Press Complaints Commission at Somerset
House in February 2001, a Bolland-orchestrated
event, Camilla nattered away quite happily with
the people waiting outside. After the party she
waited in her car for Tom Parker Bowles who was
still inside the building and taking a long time to
come out. She tutted and rolled her eyes in mock
impatience and wound down her window to talk
to a woman standing nearby, 'I'm waiting for my
son. He'll probably be ages – chatting up the girls
I should think,' she said. The woman was very
pleased. Camilla had cosied up to her, woman to
woman, the girlfriend of the heir to the throne,
confiding, mother to mother, with Mrs Jo Public.

During one of Prince Charles's arty weekends
at Sandringham, when he was handed a bunch
of flowers by a member of the public outside
Sandringham Church, he promptly passed them
straight on to Camilla, making it quite clear that
he would in the future like Mummy's subjects to
give their flowers to his girlfriend.

Few people actively object to Camilla any more, except perhaps Sophie Wessex, who gets upset if Mrs Parker Bowles doesn't curtsey to her. The hate mail from the public is sparse and for months on end non-existent, really only increasing on the anniversary of Diana's death when the Princess worshippers stick their misty, tear-stained poems to the railings outside Kensington Palace. Meanwhile, opinion polls demonstrate that fewer and fewer people object to the idea of Camilla and Charles marrying, although even fewer like the idea of her ever becoming queen. And what does the Queen think? The answer to this question varies, depending on who you speak to. One friend of Camilla's maintains that the Queen is very keen on Camilla as a person but thinks that marriage is a bad idea, because it will just complicate the God-awful mess created by that 'twit of a son of hers'. Someone else, on the other hand, someone closer to Charles's lot than the Queen's lot, says, 'The Queen can't stand Camilla these days. She can't even consider a marriage taking place. She just wishes Charles had got on with it and married Camilla 30 years ago and then none of this would have happened. She holds Camilla responsible for everything. The Queen doesn't speak to her. There is no small talk. She didn't even talk to her at the Jubilee parties. She has her at functions but only under sufferance. She has reluctantly conceded that the public have come around to the idea that Camilla will be part of royal life but that is as far as she will go.'

In May 2001, a biography of the Duke of Edinburgh by Graham Turner revealed that the Duke was happy that Charles had at least managed to remain faithful to Camilla, although even this looked in doubt when in 2004 rumour emerged that he had been having an affair, (that Camilla apparently knew about) with his friend the Marchioness of Duoro.

In July 2001 Prince Charles gave an interview to Mary Riddell of the *Daily Mail* and when she asked him if he was going to marry Camilla, he replied extremely Charles-ishly, 'Will I be alive tomorrow? Who knows what the good Lord has planned. You can't be certain about anything. I don't know. I just think it is important, particularly as I get older, to think about the journey that's coming next.' The journey that came next was from Highgrove to a Tetbury primary school summer fête and, while Charles was talking to a small girl, probably asking her how far she had come, a newspaper reporter pestered him about his marriage plans. 'Oh do leave me alone!' he snapped.

But, of course, we won't. Few people feel sorry enough for Prince Charles to leave him alone, especially since he still apparently wants to be our king, especially not after Diana and especially when they hear that he is so spoilt and prone to tantrums and sulks that even his friends have described him as badtempered, weak, self-righteous, petulant and self-centred. He is, we hear, a man who holds himself in such high esteem that he has someone, apparently his former valet, Michael Fawcett, to hold a urine specimen jar in place while he fills it.

This lovely fact emerged during the Burrell trial in 2003, (he was accused of stealing letters, keepsakes, personal things belonging to the Princess of Wales. The trial collapsed and it was generally accepted that he should never have been prosecuted in the first place – another palace farce.) There were many other puzzling aspects, but perhaps the regularity with which Charles was required to fill a specimen jar at all was one of the biggest. Diana is said to have suggested that Prince Charles had an "unhealthy relationship with a servant" but in 2003 it also emerged that the unhealthiness of the relationship had more to do with alleged homo-sexual acts. A former palace servant called George Smith claimed that not only had he, himself been homosexually leapt upon by another former palace servant but that he had also seen Prince Charles up to no good with the same former palace servant, who he claimed had raped him. The goings-on in the life of the Queen's heir made Camilla's beloved *Eastenders* look like the *Teletubbies*.

That George Smith was suffering from post traumatic stress disorder and alcoholism from his time serving in the Falklands, coupled with the sheer outrageousness of his allegations, meant that no one much believed him. Nevertheless, St James's Palace, (or Clarence House as it was by then) made the usual botch of things with Sir Michael Peat, Prince Charles's Private Secretary denying the allegations on the Prince's behalf – a foolish thing to do given that no newspapers or broadcasters were allowed to name the allegations anyway; although of course the rumours were spinning round the internet chat-rooms like nobody's business. The lowest point came when Mark Bolland, with his new pundit's hat on, wrote a piece in the *News of the World* describing how

Sir Michael Peat had phoned him in 2002, while he was on holiday in Tuscany, to ask 'Do you think Charles is bisexual?'

'I was astonished at Sir Michael's question. I told him that the prince was emphatically not gay or bisexual,' wrote Bolland.

Charles himself was away during all of this scurrilousness – on his official visit to India without Camilla. On his return he was told quite firmly by Sir Michael that this was one of those, all too frequent, times when his non-negotiable girlfriend would have to take a back seat.

It is unlikely, as some royal commentators suggested, that Camilla believed for a moment that any of what George Smith was claiming was true and just as she had advised Charles more than a decade before not to confess his adultery to Dimbleby, so she advised against Peat denying these allegations. She is wise, quiet and steadfast Camilla.

Her old life – the country house, the pruning, the dog hair – is well behind her now. She is recognised as Charles's partner and as such is well and truly a part of the court which so many who have worked within describe as medieval. Camilla has her 'people' and Charles has 'his'. Often they spin against each other, just as Charles's 'people' spun against Diana's in the past. There are those who say that what Camilla wants Camilla gets, but equally there are those who say that Charles listens to Sir Michael Peat, who was handed down to him from his mother, and if Peat says Camilla should not be tagging along on an official visit, then she won't be, and will have to satisfy herself with choosing the colour of the pelmets in the Clarence House drawing-rooms. Camilla is said to find this exclusion from Charles's public life 'totally humiliating', and will often decide to retire hurt – which means heading off to Highgrove on her own for a few days.

And then, sometimes, when she is really determined, she does get her way: she is not going to miss out on the extravaganzas, the starry, fashion-themed charity benefits, sitting next to Elton and Donatella.

Meanwhile, William Hill are offering even money on Charles and Camilla marrying before the end of the decade. They think it is highly probable, although they won't be paying out until the whole thing is done and dusted. 'Manchester United might be ten points clear in the league but you wouldn't pay out until the final whistle,' analogised a William Hill spokesman.

What does Rowan Williams, the Archbishop of Canterbury, think? Like the Queen, he hasn't made his thoughts public, but we do know that he believes in encouraging debate on contentious issues such as homosexuality, the role of women, disestablishment and marriage for divorcees – like Prince Charles and Camilla.

And his predecessor, the old Archbishop of Canterbury, George Carey, is said to be on Charles's side about a morganatic marriage – one in which Charles could marry Camilla but she would have no royal title.

If she does marry him, what will she be called? Christopher Wilson asserts that it definitely won't be Duchess of Cornwall as everyone had assumed, because this title is being saved for William's use, (should he marry before his father becomes king). Wilson thinks Camilla might well be called The Duchess of Rothesay. Whatever they decide, she certainly can't be Mrs Windsor. Mrs Windsor makes her sound like the bank manager's wife and the Duchess of Windsor makes her sound like Wallis Simpson – and think of all the upset she caused.

George Carey is, incidentally, quite good

friends with Charles and Camilla; he and his wife Eileen live quite near either Highgrove and they were there the night before Rowan Williams's enthronement in February 2003.

After Diana's death, George Carey met often with Camilla. Their conversation apparently revolved around what Camilla's status should be if the Queen should die and Prince Charles become a king with a co-habiting partner.

Charles and Camilla are known to have taken Anglican communion together at Highgrove, and in January 2000 there were indignant exclamation marks alongside a report that the Bishop of London, Richard Chartres, had spent the night at Highgrove, 'with Charles and Camilla under the same roof!'

The Bishop was there to bless what Charles calls the 'Sanctuary', a summerhouse where he goes for quiet contemplation. The Prince craves time alone and has taken to spending a lot of time in the Sanctuary. The surroundings are apparently plain and spartan and, one friend reports, 'Whenever we phone these days the butler says he is in the Sanctuary and asks us to call back. It is a very holy place to Charles, quite the most important retreat. It is also where he wants to be buried, side by side with Camilla.'

And what does Camilla do when Charles disappears to his Sanctuary? Her life is very much in London these days, she has friends to lunch and supper at Clarence House, she has her own little court to reign over. Her friend Virginia Carington, the old flat-mate from No 1 Stack House in Ebury Street, the one who used to put up with Camilla's endearing mess, helps out with organising her life. Camilla has a few of her own official engagements, usually connected to her work for people with osteoporosis. She has been made patron of St John, Smith Square, a concert venue, and when she turns out with Prince Charles at Sandringham she has her hand kissed and elderly folk shake with excitement.

When Camilla and Charles stay at Birkhall, as they often do, she takes part in local community functions, once achieving a 'highly commended' at a show for some flowers she picked from the Birkhall gardens. 'It was very nice,' said a show organiser, 'she did well for a first-time entrant.'

There was a time when she sat in on Prince Charles's six-monthly diary meetings, but Sir Michael Peat has put a stop to that – she had been known to be quite bossy. However, Camilla did get to sit in on the interviews for a new spin doctor when Paddy Harverson was appointed in 2003.

Other than that, she seems to be perfectly happy walking a few paces behind Charles, close enough to breathe the same air. Someone who is close to both of them predicts that they will only marry when it is all right with Prince William and Prince Harry, and the feeling is that those two young men have had enough in their young lives to cope with without any further complications. Prince Harry, especially, is a worry – if he smokes a joint, the world, as well as his father and his grandmother, gets to hear about it. 'You couldn't blame him if he was a bit messed up,' said the friend, 'and Charles and Camilla will wait until Harry is a bit more sorted out before they make any more changes in their lives.'

There is a joke, often told in Northern comedy clubs, about the man on his deathbed who tells his wife, 'Whatever has happened, you have always been there; by my side.' He goes on to list the bad things that have happened to him in his life and with each one, over and over again, he turns his head on his pillow and says to his wife, 'You were there then, as always, by my side.' And when he reaches the end of the list, his voice shifts from pathos to anger and he turns his head on his pillow one last time and says to his wife, 'Darling, you are an effing jinx.'

Camilla has always been there by Charles's side, and perhaps she has been an effing jinx. If it weren't for Camilla, he might have made a better choice of bride. If it weren't for Camilla, his bride might not have been running from the paparazzi in Paris the night she died. That Diana did die was bad enough, but that was and never will be the end of it for Prince Charles or Camilla – if Diana hadn't died, the Morton tapes would never have been broadcast, Burrell would never have written his tawdry book, and George Smith's lewd allegations would have been largely ignored.

And you can be sure there will be more like this: more things to dog Prince Charles. These things understandably depress him and they always will. Camilla has to deal with that and, like a loyal wife, she has always been there, these days legitimised to some extent by the fact that she at least lives in the same house. She has well and truly outdone Alice Keppel – she has gone the distance. Would Wallis Simpson still be hanging around after all these years unmarried, not officially recognized, compared to a horse and a haddock? Which proves just one thing, whatever kind of a person Camilla Parker Bowles is – adorable, as Jilly Cooper says, good fun, as so many of her friends say, a good mother, an excellent sex-mother, manipulative, unfeeling, scheming, raunchy, all those things – she is also constant. Who knows if she has always been in love with Charles or he with her? Who knows if they are still in love with each other? If they aren't, there is nothing they can do about it now. They are locked together: someone has died, two boys have lost their mother, the monarchy has been threatened... he can't dump her and she can't dump him. Rumours flit around like troublesome insects: that Charles has a rota of socially smart women at St James's – the Marchioness of Duoro being just one of them – a veritable harem, in which Camilla is queen and the others handmaidens. Another shockingly scurrilous rumour, put about by someone in the Knightsbridge set, is that Camilla and Dodi Fayed were once an item.

But these are the kinds of stories that circulate when only a very small handful of inner-circle dwellers knows the truth. The happy thought is that Camilla and Charles are locked together in love with each other; that they have loved each other constantly for 30 years; and that, if Charles were ever asked, on the eve of his marriage to Camilla, whether they were *still* in love, his reply would be absolute – it could never be that hurtful and obfuscating, 'Whatever love means'.

BIBLIOGRAPHY

A Greater Love – Charles & Camilla, Christopher Wilson. Headline, 1994

Camilla, Her True Story, Caroline Graham. John Blake Publishing, 2001.

Previous Engagements, Bruce Shand. Michael Russell, 1994.

The Prince of Wales, Jonathan Dimbleby. Warner Books, 1994, revised 1998.

Diana, Julie Burchill. Weidenfeld and Nicolson, 1998; paperback, Orion Books, 1999

Mrs Keppel and her Daughter, Diana Souhami. Harper Collins, 1996

Diana Her True Story – In Her Own Words, Andrew Morton, Michael O'Mara Books Ltd, 1997

The Windsor Knot – Charles and Camilla and the Legacy of Diana, Christopher Wilson. Pinnacle Books, 2002

ACKNOWLEDGEMENTS

Thanks to: Tanja James, research; David Jenkins and Elfreda Pownall, inspiration; Aurea Carpenter and Rebecca Nicolson at Short Books; Lucy Tuck at the *Sunday Telegraph*. And most profuse thanks to my staunchly royalist mother-in-law, Suzanne.

Rebecca Tyrrel is an award winning writer and columnist for the Sunday Telegraph. She is also the author of Days like These (Macmillan). She lives in London with her husband and their son.